DESTINED TO BE GREAT, BUT TIE DOWN

By

Daramola Joel Odunayo

Tel: 08033275896, 07028206482

ISBN: 9798368246475

Published by
CHRIST THE REDEEMER'S MINISTRIES
1-9, Redemption Way, P.M.B. 1088, Ebute Metta, Lagos,
Nigeria.

Unless otherwise stated, all scriptural quotation are from the Authorized King James Version of the Holy Bible.

Printed in Nigeria by: **CRM PRESS**
KM 46 Lagos-Ibadan Expressway, CRM Shopping Complex,
Back of Old Auditorium, Redemption Camp,
Tel: 08077833792, 08069452037
E-mail: crmpress@yahoo.com

Table of Content

Born Great But Tie Down

There is an evil which I have seen under the sun, as an error which proceeded from the ruler:

Folly is set in great dignity, and the rich sit in low place.
Eccl 10:5-6

DEDICATION

This book is dedicated to our Jesus Christ my savior,
Holy Spirit my senior partner in life and ministry and my heavenly Father the Almighty God (YAHWE) and to my father in the Lord, Pastor E. Adeboye

ACKNOWLEDGEMENT

I appreciate the costly efforts of Everyone who at different stage contributed immensely to the success of this book.

Preamble Introduction

Ex 1:5-22
And all the souls that came out of the loins of Jacob were
seventy souls: for Joseph was in Egypt already.
6 And Joseph died, and all his brethren, and all that
generation.
7 And the children of Israel were fruitful, and increased
abundantly, and multiplied, and waxed exceeding mighty;
and the land was filled with them.
8 Now there arose up a new king over Egypt, which knew not
Joseph.
9 And he said unto his people, Behold, the people of the
children of Israel are more and mightier than we:
10 Come on, let us deal wisely with them; lest they multiply,
and it come to pass, that, when there fillet out any war, they
join also unto our enemies, and fight against us, and so get
them up out of the land.
11 Therefore they did set over them taskmasters to afflict
them with their burdens. And they built for Pharaoh Treasure
cities, Pithom and Raamses.
12 But the more they afflicted them, the more they multiplied
and grew. And they were grieved because of the children of
Israel.
13 And the Egyptians made the children of Israel to serve
with rigour:
14 And they made their lives bitter with hard bondage, in
mortar, and in brick, and in all manner of service in the field:
all their service, wherein they made them serves, was with
rigour.
15 And the king of Egypt spake to the Hebrew midwives, of
which the name of the one was Shiphrah, and the name of the
other Puah:
16 And he said, when ye do the office of a midwife to the
Hebrew women, and sees them upon the stools; if it be a son,

then ye shall kill him: but if it be a daughter, then she shall
live.
17 But the midwives feared God, and did not as the king of
Egypt commanded them, but saved the men children alive.
18 And the king of Egypt called for the midwives, and said
unto them, Why have ye done this thing, and have saved the
men children alive?
19 And the midwives said unto Pharaoh, Because the Hebrew
women are not as the Egyptian women; for they are lively,
and are delivered ere the midwives come in unto them.
20 Therefore God dealt well with the midwives: and the
people multiplied, and waxed very mighty.
21 And it came to pass, because the midwives feared God,
that he made them houses.
22 And Pharaoh charged all his people, saying, Every son
that is born ye shall cast into the river, and every daughter ye
shall save alive.
KJV

COME OUT OF WIDOW HOUSE

Ex 3:7-10. 7 And the LORD said, I have surely seen the affliction of my people which are in Egypt, and have heard their cry by reason of their taskmasters; for I know their sorrows;
8 And I am come down to deliver them out of the hand of the Egyptians, and to bring them up out of that land unto a good land and a large, unto a land flowing with milk and honey; unto the place of the Canaanites, and the Hittites, and the Amorites, and the Perizzites, and the Hivites, and the Jebusites.
9 Now therefore, behold, the cry of the children of Israel is come unto me: and I have also seen the oppression wherewith the Egyptians oppress them.
10 Come now therefore, and I will send thee unto Pharaoh, that thou mayest bring forth my people the children of Israel out of Egypt.KJV

When the wind blows it moved you to arise against retardation and stagnation.

How do you feel when your contemporaries are elevated to the next level while you are left behind?

some people have been on the same level in the office for four to five years. Now imagine being on a spot for over 400 years! For that whole period, the Israelites were tied down by forces they could not challenge. They recorded no form of movement. They kept working as slaves but could not move forward or upwards. At best, they wandered about in circles. They remained on the same spot physically, financially and mentally. They remained underdogs for centuries. But when God was to arise and break their yoke of stagnation,

They moved forward physically, mentally, emotionally, spiritually and financially.

Have you been on the same spot for long? Has it been all motion but no movement? Has your lineage experienced an invisible ceiling over the progress of members of your family? The situation of stagnation shall be broken today in Jesus name. What members of your family could not achieve in previous generations shall be achieved by you.
the siege over your progress shall be destroyed, sooner than you expect, you shall be eating in promotion. That promotion that was denied you for years shall be delivered to you on a platter of gold as you read this book with faith.

1 king 18:1, people only spend 40 days in widowhood but Elija spent 3years

Widow house is a spiritual Slave Market or Spiritual House Arrest where demonic caretaker is supervising or controlling the affair of your life. In these sentences i will like to explain five coded word here better.

Widow house {unknowns demonic widow house}- is where you live but no progress at all, but whenever
you love to move out of this kind you will be experiencing financial difficulties; when you are financially buoyant, you will be experiencing difficulties in getting an accommodation of your choice. Many times you will say "lets from here move to our own dream house". Example: Elijah At the Widow's House for three and half year he has massage but no pulpit, only one type of food, he can't go out. 1King 17:8-24, 18:1-4. You are coming out!!!

Satanic Slave Market - Genesis 30:25-31. Jacob work for Laban for 14 years without having anything to show for it except food and cloth just like many people today are enriching business owners. When they tender their resignation letters, then the management decides on promotion and negotiation of salary and allowances.

Spiritual House Arrest - Matthew 21:1-5, Eccl. 10:15, a lot of things can tie people down i.e. Sickness, promises, pregnancy, evil prophecy, poverty etc. House arrest is a spiritual disconnect and disengagement from helper and profitable business, when you are busy doing nothing!

Demonic caretaker - note house caretakers are not the owner of the houses in their care not even living there but dictates or suggest to tenants and landlord on high rent fee to the owners. This happens at the spiritual realm:

Elijah at the Widow's House. 1 king 17:8-24,18:1-
Mephibosheth at Ziba House. 2 Samuel 9:3-13.
Gideon under the Oak tree. Judges 6:11-14.
Japheth in the Land Of Toab. Judge 11:1-11.
Samson in a Rock Etom. Judge 15:8.
Moses in the Land of the Medianite. Exodus 3:7-22.
Jacob at His In-Laws House. Genesis 30:25-30.
Zachariah at Inner Circle. Zechariah 3:1-10.
International tied down as local champion. Matthew 21:1-9.
Spiritual house arrest. Eccles. 10:15.
Until you prepare for war against the spirit of limitation and not accept it as your cross. Loose Him And Let Him Go!!! Says the lord.

YOU MUST BREAK THAT LIMIT

Overcoming your limitation in the land of your prosperity and abundance

...for you can acquire what you desire, if you don't retire but you perspire as you re-fire because you have a MESIAH that will let all your enemy plans backfire because His reign never expire.

Dear friend from the time of Adam till now there is limitation everywhere, those that have Jesus (THE MASTER KEY), the limitation will give way, Psalm 114:1-end, Act 5:1-5

WHAT IS A LIMITATION?

Delay, blindfold, boundary of area i.e. Maximum or minimum amount allowed, fruitlessness, hindrances, farthest point, degree, amount, boundary, especially one that cannot or should not be passed or exceeded, restriction, a feature or circumstance that restricts what can be done .

Typical example is a Gardner who planted a beautiful flower in his garden, water it to grow. With this you will think he love it, but whenever it grows higher than the expected height the same man will cut it in the name of trimming.

So many people pretend as if they love you but never want you grow or outgrow them. This month you shall overtake them.

WHAT DOES A LIMIT DO?

It let your mate outrun you; it wastes your time and life. It cripples your intelligence, turns able men to disables; it reduces the level of your relationship with GOD.

WHY MANY ARE LIMITED

Fear, Lack of VISION, ignorance, operating under a curse, satisfaction with present position, confusion, tiredness, wrong location, disobedient, lack of faith, not ready to sacrifice, lover of pleasure, education, environment, social life, family backgrounds, not ready to improve oneself, etc.

WHAT ARE THESE THINGS THAT LIMIT PEOPLE?

Sin, Greed, Envy, Jealous, Unforgiveness, NO Vision, Love of Sleep/ Food/ Money and Pleasure, Age, level of education, Worldly Wisdom, Impatience, Anger, Unable to control your sex urge, etc.

EXAMPLES OF PEOPLE EXPERIENCED LIMITATION ESAU, Hebrew 12:15-16 Genesis 25:27-34,
JUDAS, Act 1:15-26,
REUBEN, 1Chronicle 5:1,

GEHAZI, 11 King 5:20-27

WAYS OUT OF LIMITATION
"And the Egyptians were urgent upon the people, that they might send them out of the land in haste; for they said, We be all dead men."(Exodus 12:12+31-33
When your turning point comes, the enemies who refused to release you for several years will be unable to endure your presence for one second

HAVE A VISION: A man without a goal will die like a goat. Vision will makes you to matter.

INVESTIGATION: Do some visibility study about your life. Are you where you supposed to be? Why or why not? Why not now?

INFORMATION: Information will lead to reformation and transformation. Lack of it will leads to deformation.

DISCONNECTION: To succeed in life there are some people you must separate from, i.e. Mr Lot, Mr Jonah, king Uzzah. If you want to walk, walk with many, if you want to run, run with few but if you want fly, fly alone)

SACRIFICE: Come out of your comfort zone, sacrifice your time, talent, money, pleasure, let go and let God, without sacrifice your prayers and labour are insufficient.

DETERMINATION: Where determination exists failure cannot dismantle the flag of success.

YOU NEED A COACH: A team of sheep led by lion will defeat a team of lions led by a sheep.

IMPARTATION: Without divine backing our physical strength is useless. Deut. 34:9

REDEDICATION AND TRANSFORMATION: Go back to God. Job 22:21-29. John 3:3-1
to whom it may consignee dangerous prayer

PRAYER POINTS

I will not abort the programme of God for my life, in Jesus' name.

Oh Lord, set my inner clock for divine appointment, in the name of Jesus.

Every power suppressing my elevation, fall down and die, in Jesus' name.

Every demonic panel set up against me, scatter unto desolation, in Jesus' name.

Every satanic padlock in my hometown working against me, I command it to be roasted, in Jesus' name.

Every fetish material directed against my progress is roasted, in Jesus' name.

Every meeting summoned against me by witchcraft, receive confusion, in the name of Jesus.

I shall laugh last, whether the enemy likes it or not, in Jesus name.

Every power keeping me low, fall down and die, in the name of Jesus.

Labour in the place of prayer not to die as a labourer!!
See you at the top!!

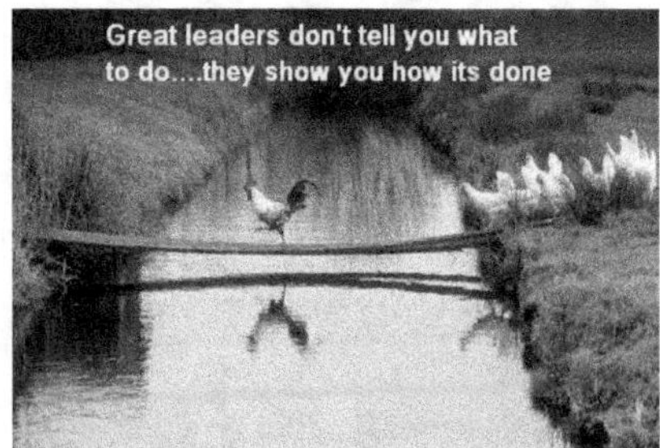

OUT OF WAITING ROOM

2 Chronicles 22:10-12, Exodus 2:1-3, Judges 16:19-22, Genesis 8:1.

What is to wait?
What is a room?
What is waiting room?
Types of waiting room?

WHAT IS WAITING ROOM?
Waiting room is delay in style
Waiting room is hold-on
Put ting someone life in pause
Suspension but not termination but without no salary
Be under embargo
Be in captivity
Free but not loose
A cage life
A typical of waiting room is archery, where an egg turns to chicken or a waste

TYPES OF WAITING ROOM?

Wait until Ps110:1=divine delay to settle you
Wait for Prov. 25:2=divine reservation
Wait in 1King17:8= divine security
Wait upon Isaiah 40:31= divine transformation
Wait to 1Sam.10:8 & 1Sam. 13-14 =divine maturity
What waiting room can turn you to?
Wait for God
Wait to be late
Wait to waste
Wait in shame Judges 16:1 & Acts 23:12
Wait in Glory Luke 24:49

MISERY OF WAITING ROOM

It is a misery to be in waiting room, many did not know until they find themselves in the web of delay that made them to be tied down unnecessary. Some power forces you to be in waiting by using this following:

It makes you to speak wrong thing that can be used to tie you down
By doing little wrong thing that noted you for demotion or belittle
Associate with failure or joining a party that will fail
By connecting you with a spouse that destiny to die barren
By cause you to fall or make a mistake at the edge of success
By misleading you to go a wrong way in order to waste your time
By making you to jump into false breakthrough e.g. buying accusation land
By weighing you down with over size load that will not let you walk faster
By wasting your major time on minor thing
To be in sickness in time of recommendation and promotion
By giving you false promotion e.g. chieftaincy that will tied you down that will not let you move to the next level
By engaging you with a struggle job that can not feed you, not let people help you and not have time to serve God wholeheartedly
What is waiting room
Waiting room is a place to wait
Waiting room is a place of forgotten or been forget
Waiting room is a place they forget you in the time of blessing
By forgetting what to do at the right time and remember when the time is not on your side
By disconnecting you in the place or time of enjoyment, it is you that know you have people but they have forgotten you

By sentence you into a strange land of waiting Eccl.10:15
To do things of reproach that made you to hid yourself in the time of honour
To feel depress and unable to explaining himself in the presence of God Neh. 6:1, they give false prophecy that will make you panic and disconnect you or using false to get truth from you
They blackmail to disconnect you from your helper Judge 14:5-6

EXAMPLE
Absalom, Esau, King Joachim, Joseph, Mephibosheth, Naomi

What are the signs of waiting room?
Disconnection
Disorderliness
Left behind
Always making mistake
Suffering for what you know not
Fear of unknown
It turns your belonging against you
Absence
Limitation of ability
Sickness and losing value

WHAT LET TO WAITING ROOM
Backsliding
Borrowing your right e.g. certificate to another fellow
When your star appear to the wicked people
Premature ceremony and testimony
Curse
Believing false prophecy
Seeking for solution in a wrong place
Refuse to accept God

OUTCOME OF WAITING ROOM

Come out but still bind John 11:45
Come out with a reproach Joshua 5:9
Come out with mixed multitude Exodus 12:38
Come out with unending war / evil pursuer. exodus 14:9
Come out with no value but with liability Ruth 1:19-22, Neh. 13:23
Come out to take over 1King 18: 1-end
Come with honour and master key Esther8:15, Exod. 4:20and Judges 11:8

7-THINGS THAT DETERMINE THE OUT COME

Preparation before you sleep Matt 25:1-10
When you refuse to be corrupted 1John 2:15, Neh.13:3
They have vision and live by faith Habbk. 2:2-4,
The word mixed with their faith Heb. 4:2
They changed by the word and not try to change the word to suit their purpose Acts 8:5
The seed of God is in them 1John 5:4&18
Their sacrifice speak for them Ps 20:1-4, Ps 50 :5

WAY OUT

Proverb 6:1-5
Prophetic word from a genuine servant of God 2King 7:1-2
The unusual sacrifice 2Samuel 24:1&15-24
When you discover yourself in the Lord Gen.27:40, Gen. 30:30 and John8:32&36
When you come out of close heaven region Matt.2:2&10, Mal.3:8-12
When you connect yourself to the right people
When you rededicate yourself and come under a new government or covenant of His son Matt.21:1-7, Gen. 35:1-2
Restitution; giving your life to Jesus Christ, holy living, attending a Bible believing Church.

Colossians 1: 3, Psalm 27: 1 - 2

PRAYER POINTS

Bless and thank God for His mercy and grace upon you.

2. Declare your decision to remain faithful to Jesus all the days of your life.
3. Renounce and break every inherited evil covenant, in Jesus name.
4. Break and loose yourself from every inherited course in Jesus name.
5. Every Satanic power monitoring my destiny, be paralyzed by fire, in the name of Jesus.
6. Let the angels of God arrest every negative words spoken against my destiny, in the name of Jesus.
7. I remove my life from the agenda of my household witchcraft, in the name of Jesus.
8. Arrows of evil limitation operating in my life, come out with all your root and die, in the name of Jesus.
9. Every ungodly convention holding for my sake scatter to desolation, in the name of Jesus.
10. I reject the calendar of death prepared for my divine potentials, in the name of Jesus.
11. Where others are failing in my family, I shall excel by fire, in the name of Jesus.
12. I remove my name from the roaster of dark agents in my family, in the name of Jesus.
13. Lord, arise and swallow every rage of poverty designed for me in your power, in the name of Jesus.
14. Every star hijacker from my place of birth, receive divine madness, in the name of Jesus.
15. You progress diverters from my past, I damage your weapon of divination by fire, in the name of Jesus.
16. Wicked broadcasters of my divine goodness fall down and die, in the name of Jesus.
17. I refuse to die the death of an unbeliever, in the name of Jesus.

18. Lord, arise and promote me by fire, in the name of Jesus.
19. Lord, accelerate my divine honor by fire, in the name of Jesus.
20. Thank God for answered prayers.

THE SIEGE IS OVER!

2Kings 6:24 -33, 7:1 - 20
What is a siege? When a life is under siege, why do enemy besiege, 7 things that siege does, what can bring siege. Etc.

May your destiny never be under siege?
I am sure you are already soaring high like eagle and pray that you will continue to fly high in Jesus name.
Eagle soars higher even the Atlantics Ocean the sea until it find himself in cage of man that his song change to. ``I believe I can fly, but unable to fly just because of human cage a siege.
If this is your case, then it means you're under a siege which must be over today.

The English word- siege is derived from the Latin word meaning to sit.
The dictionary meaning of a siege is a military blockage of a city or fortress with the intent of conquering by attrition or assault. However, as individual, we also go through a siege

which could be physical or spiritual. One can give examples of the life of Job and Joseph in the Bible.

2 Kings 6-7, the city of Samaria is under a siege. The siege lasted so long that they ran out of food; a great famine struck the city, and food prices inflated out of sight. It was so severe that a donkey's head sold for 80 shekels—the average wage was a shekel a month. Almost 7 years' worth of wages to buy a donkey's head that was considered unclean, and had almost no nutritional value. And a cup of dove's dung sold for 5 shekels! You know you're out of food when you're willing to pay 5 months wages for a cup of bird poop! The famine was so severe that women were cooking and eating their own children! It doesn't get much more desperate than that!

Another name for siege
Spiritual house arrest. Eg. Prolonged sickness, delay, suspension, disconnection
Siege is a life in a cage

I pray that God will also deliver you from every siege in your life in Jesus name.

Sign of siege life
It wastes life. Time. Resources. Opportunity
It ties down someone
It empty someone
It disconnects someone from help at large
It forces you to accept or do evil
It kills your future or glory
It wears you out
Certified and have no job
Ability without productivity
Womb without baby
Accredited workshop without client

When a life is under siege,
There will be desolation and emptiness instead of fruitfulness and abundance.
The devil intends to bring those under his dominion to the place of total elimination, desolation and waste John 10:10. God will deliver you in Jesus name.
A life under siege is synonymous with the life of a jailed person where all indispensable essentials of life and even the seemingly negligible benefits of life are cut off but God will set you free in Jesus name.
When you go from one affliction to another, as you are losing so are you binding, from one deliverance program to another, fasting to fasting, when you live the life of fear and attack, then you are under siege and you really need to seek the face of God for help.

2 Chronicles 32:22-23. In military parlance, army reconnaissance exercises and operations where military forces surround a place and cuts off its supply is what is aptly described as a siege.
When a town, a city or a country is under a siege, it is easy, sometimes effortlessly easy, to exert unhindered authority and expect complete compliance and docile submission from the captured slave-turned citizens.

When there is a siege, there is famine. Famine is physical lack of food and water which is generally economic based but it means more than that spiritually. Spiritual famine is when you are unable to pray, unable to praise God and unable to hear from God as you use to hear from him. Spiritual famine is when you live in a state of fear, your dream land is scary and everything around you looks bleak and dark. Spiritual famine is also a state of ill health and fruitlessness. Are you experiencing one sort of famine or the other in your life? I pray that God will deliver you from famine in Jesus name.

Famine can also be provoked by our sinful acts. May God have mercy upon us in Jesus name?

Why do enemy besiege

Ephesians 6:10-6:18

To besiege a city, an armed force surrounds and isolates it, while usually continuing its attacks upon it. In general, siege warfare involves bombardment (anything from, in ancient times, arrows or flaming arrows, catapulted rocks, or even catapulted corpses of plague victims to cause epidemics among the defenders, to, in modern times, artillery and "smart bombs") and cut off of supply, which causes starvation and deprivation.

It was usually only after the city surrendered, or was greatly weakened, that infantry entered.

To force you to surrender

To humiliate you

After many days, the defenders became weak because of lack of food. They were forced to eat anything that they could find including dogs, horses, mules, cats and even rats.

Their last stand was made at a point of the defences called Fort Desperate.

Through sin, the devil can bring a man under a siege, stifling out his divine blessings and spiritual strength. Such a man is converted into a spiritual robot as the devils blinds his mind and reduce him into a spiritual nonentity, 2Cor.4:4.

What can bring siege

Personal sin. Judges 6:1

Opposition. 2 king 6:24

House hold enemy. Matthew 21:21:1-

Lost of the flesh. Judges 16:1

In time of famine or siege, we need help only from God. Only God can rescue us from famine. He is the author as well as the finisher of our faith Rev 12:2. We need to trust God for help and rely totally on Him. Seek forgiveness from Him and also directions. His mercies endure for ever. Psalm 136

Desperate situation cannot be resolved desperately. We have to wait patiently on God for solution. During famine or siege, we get to a stage where we are so desperate. Job was asked by his wife to deny God and be relieved but he knew that will not bring permanent solution Job 2:9. Here, when it's just a day to the solution, some women resulted in desperate solution which eventually was regretted. Avoid taking desperate actions when you are going through challenges as solution may not come from such action rather it may lead to regret. Sometimes God's answer comes by waiting patiently. Sarah waited patiently and got answer to her problem Gen 18. In time of siege, do not play the blame game. Here the King of Israel was putting the blame on Elisha who had been of help to the king many times. Whenever we go through challenges, we always look for whom to put the blame upon. Children will put the blame upon their parents, wife upon her husband and husband upon the wife etc. Some even blame themselves and found it difficult to forgive themselves. Putting blame here and there does not solve the problem. Focusing on the famine too will not solve the problem. The answer is to focus on God that can solve all problems.

Don't give up. In times of siege people easily give up. Infact some commit suicide. Please do not give up. Every siege, every challenge has a time limit. I pray that the problems you are going through will expire today in Jesus name. The king of Israel said why should I wait upon the Lord any longer. He gave up on the Lord when the solution is just 24 hours away. So it is in the life of many of us. Are you about to give up concerning your marriage, your job, your admission and all the areas you have been trusting God on, please do not give up because the solution is already knocking on your door.

Some even go to the devil for solution after giving up on God. Laying your hands on the plough and looking back will not make you fit for Gods kingdom Luke 9:62

God can use anybody or anything to bring an end to your siege. God used four lepers here to bring the siege to an end. Do not look down on anyone or anything for the weapon of our warfare is not canal 2 Cor 10:4. With God, all things are possible. He used lepers without limbs who are already persona non grata to terrify the Syrians. I am praying that God will also fight for you and you will hold your peace. Exodus 14:14.

In time of siege, relate with God in faith. Without faith it is impossible to please God and God is a rewarder of those that diligently seek him. Heb 11:6. When the prophet said that the famine will expire in the next 24 hours, one person said, even if God opens all the windows of heaven, it is impossible. This is absolute lack of faith in God. He has forgotten that there is nothing too hard for God to do. Gen 18:14. He has forgotten that with God all things are possible Matthew 19:26. Lack of faith in God delays miracle. In time of siege we should operate with God in faith. The man paid dearly for his lack of faith because as the prophet has said, he saw it but did not benefit from it. When David was going to confront Goliath, he went in faith and defeated Goliath 2 Sam 17:37. Shadrach, Meshach and Abednego went into the fury furnace in faith and God delivered them Daniel 3:17

Take a step of faith. The lepers took a step of faith. They ventured into enemy territory. At a stage in our challenges, we also need to walk the faith we have in God. We need to put the faith into action. We need to act according to the word of God. If the lepers did not take the risk, God will not use them to terrify their enemies. You too should begin to put your faith into action and you will see what God will do for

you. Are you trusting God for the fruit of the womb, begin to prepare for a baby or for twins or triplets because God has granted your heart desire.
God terrified the Syrian. I believe all your entire enemy, this month God will terrify them and they will leave you alone. Leave the battle to God to fight for you. Remember you have no power of your own.

Spread the news. When the lepers found the spoils, they remembered that if they do not spread the news within twenty four hours, they will be in trouble. They quickly returned to Samaria with the good news. Are you also spreading the good news about Jesus Christ? Do you give testimonies about the miracles God has done and He is still doing in your life. Remember, they overcame by the blood of the lamb and the word of their testimonies. Rev 12:11. Jesus Christ commanded us to Go ye into all the world and spread the good news.

Way out

2king 7:6. Genesis 20:3. Isaiah 45:1-4
Re-examine your life, salvation
Resituate you questionable past
Go back to God in holiness, back to bethel, back to your first love
Forgive and forget
Sacrifice unto God for open door 2king 3:26-27
Invite God {hire God against your siege}
Pray-through for people to risk their life and position for your own deliverance or angelic visitation
2chronicle 11; 17-18. Act 12:5-16. 2king 7:1-8-
In conclusion, every siege has twilight. The Bible says weeping may endure for a night but joy cometh in the morning. Psalm 30:5. Your siege is over and your joy has come in Jesus name. Just begin to praise Him that is able to do exceeding abundantly above all that we ask or think,

according to the power that worketh in us. Eph 3:20. He will do your own too this month and give you total victory in Jesus name
1 Samuel 17 . Isaiah 49:25-26

PRAYER POINT

1. Every garment of bondage, catch fire, in the name of Jesus.
2. O God arise and catapult me to a greater tomorrow, in the name of Jesus.
3. Thunder of God, arise, waste my enemies, in the name of Jesus.
4. Every tree planted in my life by the strongman, die, in the name of Jesus.
5. Strongman of poverty, assigned against me, die, in the name of Jesus.
6. Every power delaying my success, die, in the name of Jesus.
7. Every power hindering my progress, die, in the name of Jesus.
8. Every strongman frustrating my breakthroughs, die, in the name of Jesus.
9. Every strongman blocking my chances, die, in the name of Jesus.
10. Every strongman diverting my blessings, die, in the name of Jesus.
11. Every power destroying my business and blocking my opportunities, die, in the name of Jesus.
12. To every strongman in charge of my case, I invade your domain and put you under arrest, in the name of Jesus.
13. I pull you down to zero level and I bind you with fetters of iron, in the name of Jesus.
14. Receive fire and brimstone after the order of Sodom and Gomorrah, in the name of Jesus.
15. I trample upon you, in the name of Jesus.

16. I come as a strongman against you and I overpower you with the blood of Jesus, in the name of Jesus.
17. I seize your weapons and smash them to irreparable pieces, in the name of Jesus.
18. I recover my stolen goods from you, in the name of Jesus.
19. Net of dark powers, release me, in the name of Jesus.
20. Power of the wicked avenger upon my life, die, in the name of Jesus.
21. Blood of Jesus, neutralize any evil blood of my parents in me, in the name of Jesus.
22. Every evil hand disturbing the programme of God for my life, catch fire, in the name of Jesus.
23. Every battle acquired from my father's house, die, in the name of Jesus.
24. Pillar of demotion, break, in the name of Jesus.
25. Every power that does not want to let me go, Lord, visit them with the ten plagues of Egypt, in the name of Jesus.
26. Every contrary wind assigned against me, backfire, in the name of Jesus.
27. Every utterance from any shrine working against me, die, in the name of Jesus.
28. Calvary covenant, arise by fire, scatter every negative covenant afflicting my life, in Jesus name.
29. Any seal of darkness upon my life, scatter, in the name of Jesus.
30. Every problem assigned to ridicule me, die, in the name of Jesus.
31. The mighty and the terrible assigned against me, die, in the name of Jesus.
32. Witchcraft decisions on my destiny, expire, in the name of Jesus.
33. I shot down any spiritual gunmen assigned against me, in the name of Jesus.
34. Every strongman resident in the heaven over my head, fall down and die, in the name of Jesus.

35. I recover seven-fold, everything that the strongman has stolen from me, in the name of Jesus.
36. Power to break the power of the strongman, fall upon me now, in the name of Jesus.
37. O thou that troubleth the Israel, the God of Elijah shall trouble you today.
38. O God arise and uproot anything You did not plant inside my life.

ENTER INTO GOD REST

ACCELERATE FROM DIVINE REFUGE TO DIVINE REST - (JEREMIAH 40:4-5, EXODUS 33:14)

When Israel went out of Egypt, the house of Jacob from a people of strange language; Judah was his sanctuary, and Israel his dominion. The sea saw it, and fled: Jordan was driven back. The mountains skipped like rams, and the little hills like lambs. What ailed thee, O thou sea, that thou fleddest? Thou Jordan, that thou wast driven back? Ye mountains that ye skipped like rams; and ye little hills, like lambs.

Tremble, thou earth, at the presence of the Lord, at the presence of the God of Jacob; Which turned the rock into a standing water, the flint into a fountain of waters.(Psalms 114)

From this bible quote we can see that a barren land exists between Egypt and Canaan. This place is called the Land of Refuge. There, no house or farm exists on it and no one desires to purchase any valuable item there because of the things they encounter there. On this land, nothing could be achieved there and no rest exists for them there. I pray, God will move you to your place of rest, in Jesus Name.

You need to examine your location; to determine whether you are in the Land of Refuge or the Land of Rest, which is the land of fulfilment. Those who live in the land of refuge are called the refugee.

Elijah spent 31/2 year in the Land of Refuge at Zarephat (the widow's) house. In the Land of Refuge there is no promotion rather when celebration comes, it is simply tolerated. There are several messages to preach but there is no pulpit to deliver the message.

Naomi lost her personality in the Land of Refuge. She lost her husband and her two sons (Ruth 1:1-6). Even Ruth and Orpah lost their husband in their Land of Refuge.
I pray for you today that anything you have lost in the Land of Refuge, God will recover them all for you in Jesus Name.
When a marriage is made on the basis of a Land of Refuge all is management, lack of satisfaction and all is simply endurance instead of enjoinments.
The home would be full of obstacles, hindrances and any relief package called miracle is wasted by scavengers who pretend to offer friendship.
It is important to understand that all these things are not God's plan for your life.

In Gen. 19:1-29, we are told of how Lot and his family lost their properties in the city of Sodom and Gomorrah. Although they escaped the destruction, they remained with the attributes of the Land of Refuge, to an extent that the sons made the father drunk so that he fell into a deep sleep. (Gen 19:30-38). This tells us to be warned; never should we manifest the refuge lifestyle in the Land of Rest.

We have star-killers in the land. Matthew 2:1-18, of refuge where world champions are become local champion. Matthew 21:1-3.

In Judges 16:5-22 some people hired Delilah to cripple Samson's Ministry.

I pray that any Hired assassin sponsored against you will die single-handedly this month in Jesus Name. Jere. 20:11, Psalm 125:3.

AT THE CITY OF REFUGE
(Number 35:6, Joshua 20:2-9)
Is the city of complain and not complaint
The land of endurance and not enjoyment
Where there is confusion because people refuse to be orderly.

What leads people to the land of refuge?
Where you are seen as a refugee.
Many were born there (Exodus 2) – Moses
Household wickedness (Judges 11:1-8)
Parental evil. (Lamentation 5:7)
Enemy attack (Acts 8) – Philip at Samaria.
Financial meltdown (Ruth 1) – Naomi
When the evil man rules (1Kings)— 17:1-10
Where you are enticed by what you see (Gen. 13:11-12) – Mr Lot
Where you are disconnected from God (Judges 16:15-20)
Where you flee away from Gods' assignment (Jonah 1)
Because of mixed multitude or Sin

Divine Rest Is Your Birth-right
Between the Land of Egypt and Canaan is the Land of Refuge. The tragedy of life is that majority die in the land of refuge, without getting to the Promise Land.

What to do to get to the Land of Rest (Fulfilment)

From reading Hebrew 4:2-4, we come to an understanding that we should let the massage take change in your life. Don't change the message, let the message change you. The only thing that Jesus says is permanent and settled is God word (Matt. 5:17)

Go back to you Bethel Gen. 35:1-8, return back to your foundation. Why did you join the Church? Why did you give your life to Jesus? (Have you given your life? Or just associated with Jesus?).
Repair your broken altar (1King 18:30-38)
Total obedience even when it looks foolish but sinful (Isaiah 1:19)
Believe and always think of good report (Phil.4:8-9)
Forget the past and look for the truth (Heb.12:1-2, Phil. 3:10-14)
Don't settle for average because average is the best among the worst and worst of the good. The choice is yours.

Refuge or Rest? ARE YOU A REFUGEE OR A CITIZEN?

Removing blockages operating at the edge of miracles call siege!!

PRAYER POINT

I confess my sins of exhibiting occasional doubts.

2. Let the angels of the living God roll away the stone blocking my financial physical and spiritual breakthroughs in the name of Jesus.
3. I bind every spirit manipulating my beneficiaries against me in the name of Jesus.
4. I remove my name from the book of seers of goodness without appropriation in the name of Jesus

5. Let God arise and all the enemies of my breakthrough be scattered in Jesus name.
6. let the fire of God melt away the stones hindering my blessings in the mighty name of Jesus.
7. Let the cloud blocking the sunlight of my glory and breakthrough be dispersed in the name of Jesus.
8. All the secrets of the enemy in the camp of my life that are still in darkness let them be revealed to me from now in the name of Jesus.
9. All evil spirits masquerading to trouble me be bound in the name of Jesus.
10. Lord let me not put unprofitable and heavy load upon myself in the name of Jesus.
11. All the keys to my goodness that are still in the possession of the enemy Lord give them to me.
12. Open my eyes O Lord and let my ways get not darkened before me.
13. All my sweats on the affairs of my life will not be in vain in the name of Jesus.
14. Let the pregnancy of good things within me not be aborted by any contrary power in the name of Jesus.
15. Lord, turn me to untouchable coals of fire.
16. Lord, let wonderful changes begin to be my lot from today.
17. Lord, remove covetousness from my eyes.
18. Lord, fill the cup of my life to the brim.
19. Let every power stepping on my goodness receive the arrow of fire of God now in the name of Jesus.
20. I reject every spirit of the tail in every area of my life in the name of Jesus. I claim the head.
21. Thank God for the victory.

RELEVANT OR OUTDATED

Renewal in the Spirit
And Jesus increased in wisdom and stature, and in favour with God and man.
Luke 2:52,
the righteous shall flourish like the palm tree: he shall grow like a cedar in Lebanon…Those that be planted in the house of the LORD shall flourish in the courts of our God…They shall still bring forth fruit in old age; they shall be fat and flourishing;
Psalm 92:12-14
And be not conformed to this world: but be ye transformed by the renewing of your mind, that ye may prove what is that good, and acceptable, and perfect, will of God.
Romans 12:2,
And be renewed in the spirit of your mind;. And that ye put on the new man, which after God is created in righteousness and true holiness.. Wherefore putting away lying, speaks every man truth with his neighbour: for we are members one of another… Be ye angry, and sin not: let not the sun go down upon your wrath. Neither gives place to the devil.
Ephesian 4:23,
Let him that stole steal no more: but rather let him labour, working with his hands the thing which is good, that he may

have to give to him that needed... Let no corrupt communication proceed out of your mouth, but that which is good to the use of edifying, that it may minister grace unto the hearers...And grieve not the Holy Spirit of God, whereby ye are sealed unto the day of redemption... Let all bitterness, and wrath, and anger, and clamour, and evil speaking, be put away from you, with all malice:
Colossian 3:10,
And have put on the new man, which is renewed in knowledge after the image of him that created him:
Titus 3:5. Not by works of righteousness which we have done, but according to his mercy he saved us, by the washing of regeneration, and renewing of the Holy Ghost;

Relevant means correct or suitable for a particular purpose
Out-dated means old fashioned and therefore not as good or as fashionable as something modern.
Today relevant that refuse to be grow or upgraded will later become tomorrow out dated.
Where there is mass production, low quality is order of the day.
Note: You can grow up without losing taste.
You can't be loaded and not be needed, if you are loaded and not be needed ask yourself what stuff has you be loaded with. If it is junks you may not be needed in the party but in the garbage.
But I know you are a vessel (TREASURE BOX) and not a container (DUST BIN).

If you have what people need, they will patronize you. This simple truth is what separates people into classes. In the world, there are problems and every problem is calling for solution. If you are a solution provider, you will never lack provision. He who has the solution gets the promotion. If you are not needed, then it is because you cannot provide solution to people's problems. Know that no one will give you a chance; you have to take charge but taking charge is not by muscle, it is by input. When you make input, your impact will show.

You cannot be making impact and not be recognized. You cannot be affecting your environment positively and not earn respect. So the question is, what is in and what are you loaded with? Life is like the computer, it displays only what is fed into it. Feed yourself if you want people to feel you. There are good jobs everywhere and there are vacant positions at the top begging for occupiers. It is the bottom that is congested, the top is free, but to get there, you must do extra work.

Sit down and work on yourself. Unskilled labourers are not well paid anywhere in the world. It is when your type is rare that your salary will be high. SO, settle down early to specialize. Be a consultant or an expert on a particular field.

Be a service provider. The money you need is tied to the goods and services you can provide. People do not care whether you are a man or a woman, young or old, tall or short, black or white but if you can provide them with what they need, you will become their 'source'.

TO BE RELEVANT FOR LIFE CONSIDER THESE THING

YOUR ENVIRONMENT MATTERS
FOR YOUR ENVIRONMENT DETERMINES YOUR EMPOWERMENT

Your location will determine your allocation and association
When the world number one dog died in February 2004, it was major worldwide headline news. Yes, the dog of U S president, George Bush called, 'Spot" passed away. Indeed,

if there was a paradise or heaven for animals, Spot is there eating the fattest bone and living in a mansion. This 15-year-old English springer breed had a privileged life, died a privileged death and got a burial befitting a king. When he died, the White House issued a statement and Spot was flown all the way from Washington D.C to Texas possibly Air Force One, the presidential jet for special burial. Oh! Indeed, all animals are equal, but some are more equal than others! How many dogs do you see knocked down by vehicles on streets of Africa daily?

If Spot lived in Africa or in an underdeveloped country, it would probably end up in a pepper soup pot as '404' (the local name for sourced dog) or probably used as a sacrifice to the deities. Indeed, your location can determine your promotion. Yes, indeed, your environment can determine your empowerment! Indeed, the Spot you are, the kind of people you associate with, the kin of words you hear, the kind or music you are listening to, the kind of books you read, the kind of news you listen to, determine your eventual fortune or misfortune in life and ministry. Every location that limit your ability must release you today MATTEW 21:1-7

GOOD CHARACTER WILL BRING GOOD REPUTATION

You cannot grow tall where your character is low. Reputation is what people think you are but your character is who you are. Too many pretend to be what they are not. What they are not at home is different from what they are at work. If you are really want to know a man; ask his wife and if you want to know the true person of a woman; ask her husband also.

People do all they could to perfect their reputation while their characters remain horrible. If you know the story of many so called celebrated men after their death, you will be amazed at the level of their shoddy activities. Many illegitimate affairs, unclaimed and unwanted children, secret/private bank accounts and properties etc. in which many get involved in are discovered after their death.

Never vouch for anybody expect you know him/her very well. The truth is; if you work to build a good character, your reputation will be intact. Have self-respect. If you do, certain insults will not come near you. There are places you must not be found, there are languages that should not be heard from you and words that must not be in your mouth if you have self-worth.

MANAGEMENT YOUR TIME

TAKE TIME TO MAKE TIME If i know how you manage your time, then i can tell you what your financial life will be. One of the greatest strategies of an average black man is lack of respect for time. People talk of “African time”. Africans do not have a different time from the rest of the world. God gave all human beings 24 hours a day. So, we must be disciplined.

I have never met a poor person who valued time neither have I met a successful person who did not valued time.
Time is the only thing God gave man and gave it to all of us equally. It is your duty as well as mine to use the time given us to achieve good things. Whatever you have, is achieved by time and whatever you do not have, the reason is that you did not give it enough time.

One of the greatest challenges of today church is time management; Pastor believes the time is too short, and member hope the service is too long.
Even does that complain about time when it come to their time to testify they still love to waste time not deliberate, but

can we say the church fail to plan or have a standard in the name of HOLY SPIRIT took over the time of service. Time is a blank and balance cheque that God gave every human being equal.
Rich or poor get 24hour a day, how you spend your time, the end will judge.

EXPOSE TO BE MATURE

Age is in the calendar; if you do not mind it, it does not matter. Age and maturity are not the same; while age is principally a character issue, maturity is more of the mind. Maturity has to do with wisdom, character, disposition and result. It is only in Africa that people clamour for respect; all over the world, respect comes with result.

Maturity is a function of the mind. So, how developed is your mind? You may be a 40 year old still on feeding bottle or la cing diapers like a baby. This has to do with the way you think, react and handle issues. On the other hand, there are people below the age of 30 that handle life issues maturely and intelligently. It all depends on the mind.
II Timothy 2:15,

How exposed are you? Exposure is a determinant of maturity. Do you know that travelling is a form of education? That is why schools organize excursion for their pupils. If you want to see what you have never seen, go to places you have never been.

Make new contacts, do new things, meet people, take part in projects and change locations. If you are exposed you will be more matured....

Experience of life: Nothing brings about maturity in a person like the experiences of life; that is the challenges faced. Challenges have a way of making man matured. So, do not be afraid to face unpleasant situations. It is your season of abundance and lifting in Jesus name.

DON`T BE OVER COMMITED

Do not take on too many things at the same time. When you are committed to many things or to many people, your effectiveness will reduce and you may run the risk of losing your integrity. I know of people who make financial commitments in form of pledges and promises at almost all the fund raising programmes or services they attend. With so many pledge forms and limited resources at their disposal, they find it difficult to honour their pledges while the people they promised will keep sending reminder letters. At the end, such people's integrity will be questionable.

The same thing happens when you are committed to too many people. So, you must develop the ability to reject offers or invitations that will congest your life and plan.

You must also learn to do only a few things which you can do very well. Jack of all trade is a master of none, therefore be wise. When you are involved in too many things, you will be less effective in all. Reduce your activities; too many things will lead to ineffectiveness. Narrow to a few things you can do very well and be distinct on them.

Be integrity driven. Let the issue of uprightness be uppermost in your mind; let your word be your bound. Always keep to your words; do not make promises you know you won't be able to keep or pledges you won't honour. Be your best to beat the rest. I decree great level of anointing on you in Jesus name.

STOP BLAMING GAME GIVE YOUR ABILITY RESPONSIBILITY

Stop blaming people, things, circumstances, situation etc. for your adversities and reverses in life. Those who look for who to blame eventually become lame. No matter what had happened to you, no matter the disappointment or the frustration, do not blame anybody. Do not spend your entire time and life blaming people; instead get up and move on.

Regret does not translate to progress and no one move forward while looking backwards. The time you spent regretting, blaming and fighting could have been used to repackage yourself and things for a more profitable venture. Somebody might have been responsible for your yesterday's setback, but what about now? Your today is in your hands. May be then, you were young, uniformed, ignorant etc. but now, your destiny lies with you.

Do not accept your failure statue. In I Chronicles 4:9-10, Jabez's mother named him sorrow which automatically authenticates his failure; but he rejected that status and opted for a more honourable life. The truth is, whatever people call you is not as important as what you call yourself. How people see you is not as crucial as how you see yourself. Whatever you accept stays and that which you reject goes.

POWER OF ASSOCIATION

Association is vital to every man that is in pursuit and fulfillment of destiny.

Who you follow determines what follows you.
Where you stand determines how and what you view.
You company determines your accomplishment.
Your location determined your allocation.
Your position determines your possession.
Your posture determines your posterity.
The direction you face determines the attraction you make.
Your association determines your influence.

Many people are destroyed not for the evil they did but for the company The keep. Prov. 13:20. Ps. 1:1-3
Similarly, blessings and lifting's are enhanced by reason of the company we keep.
Locate your company, join your company and stick to your company to enjoy
great accomplishments

POWER OF ASSOCIATION
Association is vital to every man that is in pursuit and fulfillment of destiny.
Who you follow determines what follows you.
Where you stand determines how and what you view.
You company determines your accomplishment.
Your location determined your allocation.
Your position determines your possession.
Your posture determines your posterity.
The direction you face determines the attraction you make.
Your association determines your influence.
Many people are destroyed not for the evil they did but for the company The keep. Prov. 13:20. Ps. 1:1-3
Similarly, blessings and lifting's are enhanced by reason of the company we keep.
Locate your company, join your company and stick to your company to enjoy
great accomplishments

Stop blaming people for your predicament. No matter what was done to you and whoever did it; leave everything to God and stop apportioning blame to individuals. Jabez's prayed to God and his prayer was answered; God changed his status to a more honourable one and he moved from sorrow to honour.

What you fail to change will eventual change you. Somebody needs to change, when you refuse to change, you end up in chain of shame. That's why it is very essential to know how and what t do to make one's life better. Until you change, you cannot be in charge. Until you change, you may not have a chance and until you change, you may not remain in chains. Change breaks chains, yet many people are so reluctant to yield to it. It is an evidence of growth. Almost everything in life is constantly changing. The only thing that is permanent in life is change.

The weather changes, government changes, music, language, mode of dressing, culture, people, environment and everything around us is changing. If you refuse change, you will be left behind. By the way God made things, He has given us a clear message of the inevitability of change.

For instance, little children's shoes and dresses become smaller for them in no time. Their shoes and dresses must be changed because they are growing. Growth calls for change; where change is resisted, growth is thwarted. So, upgrade and update, if you do not upgrade, you will be downgraded and if you refuse to be updated, you will be outdated.

Only two set people in life don't change; a dead man and a fool. A dead man can`t and fool will not.

Break the old habit. Many people are hooked with some bad habits which they picked up from 'god knows where'. I know habit is difficult to break but when your will is strong. The chain will break. As you break the old habits, cultivate new ones. If there is a good idea or style you see somewhere or in someone, learn it.

We all need to learn to learn from each other; do not be too proud or old fashioned to learn new things.

If your CHURCH can`t change you change your CHURCH,
You can change your faith, Church, Friend. But don't change your God

Change with change. Do not behave as if the one thing you know is the only one that exist neither must you say your own is the best. God will put an end to all afflictions in your life. You won't know reduction on your life's endeavor in Jesus name.

Conclusion:
Are you an asset or liability to your environment? Many call themselves Christian in a church for 3 years without been baptized or joining workers. They always disturb their leader with their challenge. Many of our workers cannot be compared with someone who is 10 years old in other religion or someone that just join OPC for 30 days. Are you empty or loaded, that is why you are troubled in your dream up and down because you are not living up to heavenly standard. You need to refill yourself or charge your heavenly batteries.
Christianity is like a pot of soup that you need to warm everyday without that the soup will be sour and lose taste. Hope your salvation has not lost taste or sour?
You need to work on yourself to be relevant and not to be outdated. You need to be full of story and not only tell story of tradition.

Your fame will rise but to be famous and renowned, release the good stuff which you are loaded with. That is the key to go up. Please move to the top. By a supernatural turnaround, your long awaited miracle will happen this month in Jesus name.

PERSONAL DELIVERANCE PRAYERS
2 Corinthians 10:3-6

A. POWER AGAINST SPIRIT OF CONFUSION
I pull down the stronghold of confusion in my life in the name of Jesus.

Every seat of confusion in my life, be broken down in the name of Jesus.

Let the storm of confusion within my mind be still be still in the name of Jesus.

Every cloud of confusion within my mind be still in the name of Jesus

I reject every storm of confusion and claim a sound mind in the name of Jesus.

B. POWER AGAINST MIND DESTRUCTION

6. Every power that wants to destroy my life, I command you to be destroyed in the name of Jesus.
7. Every faulty foundation in my life, receive the fire of God in the name of Jesus.
8. I fire back every arrow of mind destruction fired into my life back to sender in the name of Jesus.
9. My mind, receive divine touch of God and be relieved in the name of Jesus.
10. Lord strengthen me in my inner mind with Your fire and Your power in the name of Jesus.

C. DELIVERANCE FROM UNCONTROLLABLE THOUGHTS

11. I pull down every stronghold of uncontrollable thought in my life in the name of Jesus.

I cast down every evil imagination in my heart in the name of Jesus.

I bring into captivity every area of my thought life to the obedient of Christ in the name of Jesus.

14. I break the power of evil remote control over my thought in the name of Jesus.
15. I seal off every doorway of evil uncontrollable thought in my life with the blood of Jesus in Jesus' name.

D. CASTING DOWN EVERY EVIL IMAGINATION

16. I scatter into pieces every evil imagination against me in the name of Jesus.
17. I command all imaginations contrary to my prayer life to be defeated in the name of Jesus.
18. I cast down and bring to naught every demonic imagination against me and my family in the name of Jesus.
19. I immune my spirit, soul, and body against every vain imagination in the name of Jesus.
20. I cast down, plunder, and frustrate every satanic imagination against my life in the name of Jesus.

E. PULLING DOWN STRONGHOLD OF IMAGINATION

21. Lord, I pull down every stronghold of the enemy over my life in the name of Jesus.
22. I pull down and roast every demonic ladder the enemy is using to climb into my life in the name of Jesus.
23. I come against every evil pronouncement made against my life in the name of Jesus.
24. I arrest and bind every satanic notebook written against my life in the name of Jesus.
25. I cancel and nullify every imagination of the enemy upon my life in the name of Jesus.

F. TAKING EVIL THOUGHTS CAPTIVE

26. I take captive every evil thought in my heart in the name of Jesus.

Blood of Jesus, cleanse my head from evil thought in the name of Jesus.

My heart, be delivered from every evil thought in the name of Jesus.

I shield my heart with the fire of God from every evil thought in the name of Jesus.

Heavenly thoughts fill my heart in the name of Jesus.

G. AUTHORITY AGAINST THE POWER THAT CONTROLS THE MIND

You my mind, in the name of Jesus, you will not push me to hell

You habitation of darkness in my heart, be desolate in the name of Jesus.

Every evil attack on my mind be defeated in the name of Jesus.

You my mind, receive the touch of the fire of God in the name of Jesus.

In the name of Jesus, I will make it in life.

H. UPROOTING THE SATANIC OPERATION FROM THE MIND

36. I command satanic table upon which he exhibits its evil in my heart to receive the fire of God in the name of Jesus.
37. Sting of death, release my mind in the name of Jesus.
38. Sting of fear and failure, release my mind in the name of Jesus.
38. I command every heavy burden in my mind to roll away and be burnt to ashes in the name of Jesus.
40. Blood of Jesus, replenish my heart in the name of Jesus.

I. PARALYZING THE STRONGMAN AGAINST MY MIND

41. You powers that corrupt my desire and my mind, be roasted in the name of Jesus.

You strongman of evil imagination paralyzing the good things in my life, be paralyzed in the name of Jesus.

43. Lord, preserve my mind with Your fire in the name of Jesus.
44. Lord, put Your laws into my mind in the name of Jesus.
45. All the good thoughts that the strongman has

paralyzed in my life, receive life, and be restored back into my life in the name of Jesus.

J. LOCATING EVIL TREE IN MIND

I locate every evil tree in my mind

I uproot every hidden evil tree in my mind in the name of Jesus.

You evil fruit in my life, die in the name of Jesus.

49. You planter of evil tree in my life be roasted in the name of Jesus.

50. Lord, begin to plant good things in my life and let the good fruits begins to manifest.

K. SPIRIT OF UNCERTAINTY 2 KINGS 7:2

I bind and cast down the spirit of uncertainty in my mind and I render its activity null and void in my life in the name of Jesus.

Holy Ghost, occupy every area vacated by the spirit of uncertainty in my mind in the name of Jesus.

53. Lord, every damage that spirit of uncertainty has done in my life be repaired and restored in the name of Jesus.

54. I refuse to give space to the spirit of uncertainty in my life in the name of Jesus.

55. I recover and possess every good thing lost to the uncertain in the name Jesus.

L. SPIRIT OF DEATH AND HELL

Throughout the days of my life, the gate of hell shall not prevail over my life in the name of Jesus.

57. You power of death and hell, release all my belongings that are under your control in the name of Jesus.

58. As for me and my house, our names will not enter the kingdom of hell in the name of Jesus.

59. You spirit of death, you will not prosper in my life in the name of Jesus.

I release the life of Christ into my life in the name of Jesus.

M. SPIRIT OF MIND WASTAGE

My mind, I command you to think right in the name of Jesus.

62. All mind control spirit, be bound in the name of Jesus.

63. You producer of evil thought in my life, somersault and die in the name of Jesus.

Holy Spirit, renew my mind to the glory of God in the name of Jesus.

Lord, soak my mind with heavenly revelations.

N. DELIVERANCE FROM FRAGMENTED MIND

66. I gather together every area of my mind that have been scattered in the name of Jesus.

67. Every area o my life and area of my mind in satanic cage, released in the name of Jesus.

68. I plead the blood of Jesus in my mind and into the whole of my life.

69. I fire back every arrow of the enemy fired into my life in the name of Jesus.

70. I command you my mind, go back to your resting place in the name of Jesus.

BORN GREAT, BUT TIE DOWN

Born great means you have opportunity to be great, but when breakthrough becomes impossible.
Judge 11: 1-16, Isaiah 38: 1, Isaiah 37:4, Lam.5:2-22, Song of Sol. 1:6 Gen. 17: 1.

Why did Abraham reach the age of 99years old before God intervene in his life?
As a Christian why did unbeliever better off than you?

Pray These Prayers Now
Father don't let my destiny expire
Oh lord I must not die before you fight for me like Naboth
Every delay to my fulfillment must be crush down
Every personality that comes into my life in order to turn the journey of 40 days to 40 years father uproot them today by fire.
Every wall of my protection that have cracked down , Lord amend it for me
Father promote me above what I shall eat
Oh Lord, break me loose from traditional limitation and unknown curse

Every illegal structure that covers the beauty of my glory crumble
Father withdraw all my benefit that is in wrong hand back to me
Every strange hand & Power of grave and Spiritual giant that is militating against me
Scatter

11. Father deliver me from the covenant of almost be there but never be there

Many never believe that enemy exist, some said they are powerless

FIVE MAJOR WAYS THROUGH WHICH THE ENEMY USUALLY TIE THEIR VICTIM DOWN

Body - through sickness, accident, paralyses, amputation etc. with these, no matter how great you are destined to be, if your body is been tied down the greatness will only remain in dream, you can ask Mephibosheth

2. Spirit - weakness, madness, emotional disorder mental retardation, anyone been tied down spiritually will just be a shadow of his glory e.g. the mad man of gaddarra, he was destined to be a governor but he governed among the demons and mad people

3. Soul - fornication, stealing, etc. if someone is being bind loutishly such will always desire to be a tail instead of being the head, love to be a beggar instead of being a giver Luke 16:20-21 Lazarus loves to eat the crumbs that fell from table that belong to the dog and that is
why dog use to attack him

4. Your belonging - your property, tools, certificate, land, promotion etc., anyone that tie your belonging down have already tied you down in disguise e.g., when your high school

graduate or university entrance examinations elude you. Instead of you to be a graduate at the age of 18 years and marry at the age of 22 years you are still searching for admission at the age of 26 years how can such a fellow be fulfilled

5. Your helper - your friend, office, church, children, wife, husband. Israel suffered extra 30 years in the land of Egypt because their helper -Moses was tied down in the land of Medianite, today you shall be set free from direct or indirect captor, you are coming out of
captivities Isaiah 14: 1- 3

HOW CAN YOU KNOW YOU ARE TIED DOWN

When breakthrough becomes impossible
When your mates over take you
When your net refuse to catch a big fish
When you pray for others and they have testimony but the prayer never work for you
When your income is always insufficient
When anyone that wants to help you always have problem
Delay, disaster, disorder, mysterious sickness and always back to square one

BIBLICAL EXAMPLE

Matthew 21: 1-6 the horse has been tied down, international champion became a local champion
Acts 3: 1-1 0 born lame from the womb
Judges 16:20-22 enemy disconnected Samson and remove his two eyes
1 Samuel 3:3-9 Samuel was tied down under a tired but not retired leader
John 9:1-9 born blind from the womb
Judges 6:11-14 Gideon was tied down with fear of unknown
Luke 13: 1 0-17 daughter of Abraham was tied down for 18 years

John 5: 1-14 infirmity tied a man down for 38 years
11 king 5: 19-27 Gehazi was tie down with leprosy because of love of money
Genesis 49:3-4 Ruben was tied down because of the hidden sin

WHAT CAN TIE YOU DOWN?

Immoral romance and sex, Hidden sin, what you love. Judges 16:5-18, House hold wickedness
Matthew 21:1-4, Inferiority, Judges 6:4-14, love of Pleasure etc.

WAY OUT
Examine yourself. (are you a child of God or just a Christian)
Restitute your way. Job 22:21-29, 2 chronicles 7:14,
Declare war. Stubbornly fight for your freedom. Jams 4:7
Go for cooperate anointing. James 5:13-20
Give your way out of limitation. Give to God, Genesis 18: 1-, 2 Samuel 24: 16-25
Holy life must follow. John 5:14
Prayer

Galatians.3:1, Acts8:9
Bewitchment power assigned against me, I rebel against you today, die, in Jesus name.
Bewitchment power of my father/mother's house assigned against my life, die.
Every curse of limitation, die, in the name of Jesus.
Every law of death over my destiny, die in Jesus name.
Every curse issued against me using the earth, break! in the name of Jesus.
Every curse issued against my life using herbal/fetish power, die, in the name of Jesus.
Every curse of vagabond anointing upon my life, be broken, in the name of Jesus.

Every curse of business failure in my life, be broken, in Jesus name.
Every curse of academic failure in my life, be broken, in the name of Jesus.
Every problem that has come into my life through the mouth gate die, in Jesus name.
Every curse of backwardness in my life, be broken, in the name of Jesus.
Every bewitchment upon my life acquired in the time of ignorance, die, in Jesus name.
The Red Sea that will make me run helter skelter, be parted, in the name of Jesus.
O Heavens declare your glory over my life, in the name of Jesus.
My life, reject every opposition to the purpose of God, in the name Jesus.
As the Lord Jesus fulfilled His destiny, so I shall fulfill mine, in the name of Jesus.
I recover my life from every witchcraft coven in the name of Jesus.
I recover my potentials from every witchcraft cage.
I recover my destiny from every form of bewitchment in Jesus name.
My life, get back on track! die, in the name of Jesus.
My correct value in life, jump out of every cage of bewitchment, in the name of Jesus.
Every opportunity to become great in all areas of my life, locate me by fire now.
Every good thing that has died in my life, resurrect now, in the name of Jesus.
I receive the touch of the Lord Jesus Christ.

RECOVER YOUR EXCHANGED DESTINY

"Praying to Recover your Exchanged Destiny"

Eccl. 10:5-7 "There is an evil I have seen under the sun, Folly is set in great dignity, while the rich sit in a lowly place, I have seen servants on horses while princes walk on the ground like servants.

There is an evil that is going on under the sun, which means there are evils being done on the face of the earth. What are these evils? You might ask! The evil that is happening is the exchange of other people's destinies. Many destinies have been exchanged. Many people are living lives that are not theirs. Many people are eating crumbs while they are supposed to eat the full bread. Many people are living unfulfilled lives. Only few people are living according to God's standard for their lives.

What is your destiny?

Destiny is the most important question of life. Once you have answered this question then you will be at rest.
Destiny begins with the question, WHO AM I?

Before I formed thee I knew thee, and before you were born I ordained thee to be a prophet.
Jeremiah 1: 5.

Everyone has been ordained unto something from birth. Yes it's so important for you to know that you did not appear here by chance, you are not a product of biology, I mean to say that you are not a biological accident you are a creature of destiny.

And until your destiny is discovered life might remain a frustration. You can be rich and still be unfulfilled, for example look at some people whom you believe then are special, they have money but still unfulfilled, that is why you can see them opening different NGOS and FOUNDATIONS to help people. Something inside them tells them that they were created for something. So they look for how to make impact.

Your destiny is a destiny of impact, but you must understand it so as to be intact and impactful.
Your destiny is so glorious that is why you are on earth. You are here for something and until that thing is discovered you remain covered.

You are not just here to go to school come out and work for somebody all your life, after that marry, give birth to children, and train them till they get married also and repeat the same cycle.

At age 12 Jesus knew who He was, remember in Luke 2 vs. 49 during His earthly ministry, when confronted by his earthly parents on why he left them sorrowing in search of Him, Jesus said that He was ABOUT HIS FATHERS BUSINESS.

IF at 20 you don't know who you are then there is a problem but thank God because its never too late to be right.
Abraham discovered his destiny at 75 and still fulfilled it no wonder we are called children of Abraham.
Joseph have his life dream at age 17 and became prime minister at age 30

David kill Goliath at age 17 and became king at age 30
Joash was 7 years old when he became king. {2 chronicle 24:1}
Moses was train to ragn as a king for 40 year also train as a shepherd in another 40 years before he discover his destiny at 80. Only lead and ragn for 40 year.
Noah discover his destiny at age 600. {genesis 7:6} and he live 950 years. {genesis 9:29}
When will you discover yours?

The only way to discover who you are is to search the-for-what He is assigned you for in scriptures. God is your creator and as your MANUFACTURER, He has a manual and that manual is the BIBLE. Why is it that people can employ every other means in discovering themselves other than the bible? But the discovery of your destiny is rooted in the word. The word is the surest word of prophecy, people that don't mind the scriptures don't mind their future.

What is destiny?
Destiny is first and foremost the original intention of God for your life, and it includes the purpose, place and program for your life.
Destiny is taken from the word destination, WHO ARE YOU,

WHAT ARE YOU HERE FOR AND WHERE YOU ARE GOING

Let me explain this very clearly, there are aspects of life which includes the business angle, political angle, the entertainment angle, career or professional sector; we also have the ministry angle.

Your destiny is what God has created you to be, right from your mother's womb;
Your destiny is God's original plan before you were created;
Your destiny is God's divine purpose before you were created;
Your destiny is God's placement in your life;
Your destiny is your assignment on earth;
Your destiny is the picture that God had in His mind before He created you;
Jeremiah 1:5 "Before I formed you in the womb I knew you", before you were born I sanctified you, I ordained you a prophet to the nations".
Before you were born, God knows already who you are,
You are specially created to become a solution to the world;
Before God gave you life; He already chose you for greatness;
You were not born by mistake; but by divine will of God;
You might be useless in the eyes of men but you are useful in the eyes of God;
You might be nobody in the eyes of men but you are somebody in the eyes of God;
You might have been rejected by men but you have been accepted by God;
It is not the name which people are calling you; but the one that the Lord has named you.
Isaiah. 43:1 "But now thus says the Lord that created thee, O Jacob, and he that formed thee, O Israel, Fear not: for I have redeemed thee, I have called thee by thy name, thou art mine"

Let look at the three kinds of destiny or Gods will for your life. But God has three wills. Romans 12 vs. 2

And be not conformed to this world , but be ye transformed by the renewing of your mind, that ye may prove what is that **GOOD, AND ACCEPTABLE AND PERFECT WILL OF GOD**

The three wills of God are the three kinds of DESTINY

THE GOOD KIND OF DESTINY;

this is the kind of destiny you see most people fulfilling. It is not Gods perfect will but it is a good will. Somebody can decide to be a doctor, lawyer, teacher, politician or most of the time business person. It is wonderful and appreciable but it is an ambition, It is a good plan but it might not be Gods master plan for your life. You might desire to build a duplex but end up building a flat; it is still very good but cannot be compared to building your desired duplex. So in the same vein it is not everybody that should go into business, but business will still be profitable.

But the difference is the fulfilment from the impact. For example look at peter one of Jesus disciples. He was a fisherman but that was not Gods perfect will for Him, but it was a good will as working is one of the will of God, but working in the area God wants you to work is equally another thing. Destiny is essentially doing what you have been designed by God to do. This is what destiny is. There is a right person for you to marry, there is a right vocation for you to practice, and even twins have separate destinies. You are not like everybody else you have a special task you have been sent to actualize. You can start at the good destiny but don't end there seek the perfect destiny. Paul in the bible one of the most profound apostles that wrote two third of the new testament, was a lawyer but that was not His destiny no wonder He was beating about the bush of life like an enraged dog persecuting Christians He was sent to build up. You will not miss Gods master plan for your life.

THE ACCEPTABLE KIND OF DESTINY;

According to Romans 12 vs. 2 this acceptable kind of destiny is the acceptable will of God. It is different from the good kind of destiny because in this kind of destiny, it becomes rather too late to fulfil Gods perfect will for your life. Because every phase of destiny is time tagged, that is there is where you must be at a particular point in time. There are specific assignment to be actualized and times and seasons are allotted. A footballer starts playing early. A forty year old man cannot desire to train for football. He is already missing the time. Remember that Ecclesiastes chapter three says there is time for everything. So if a man has been destined by God to cause some certain changes in the world as a lawyer, but did not go to school that destiny becomes impossible to be fulfilled optimally. But when that man although not schooled as a lawyer decides to fight for the right of people as an activist later on in life, this is also fulfilling His destiny acceptably not perfectly.

And it happens in all fields, as a business man there is a particular product you must sell, that means a specific line of business you must embark upon. You don't just do things you will only shine where God has designed you for. For instance the ceiling fan cannot act as a television set. It is not possible, it will be a mirage to expect that your TV set will cool you as an air conditioner, No, it will only entertain you. Do not just be a banker, be the banker, do not just be a doctor, be the doctor, do not just be a business man be the business man, do not just be a teacher, be the teacher, do not just be a pastor be the pastor, do not just be a writer be the writer. There are some books that some men have been destined by God to write so as to ease life circumstances by addressing some issues but they failed, you shall not fail your generation in the name of Jesus.

THE PERFECT KIND OF DESTINY;

This is however the ultimate but have very few people walking in it. Everybody has a glorious destiny but not everybody will fulfill it because not everybody is ready to pay the price required.

ON YOUR WAY TO YOUR DESTINY

You must know that God has opened before you a great door but there are many adversaries, 1st Corinthians 16 vs. 9. So oppositions will show up, it did for Joseph, David and even Jesus, but you must realize that every set back is only a stepping back for a higher jump. You shall jump higher in the name of Jesus. A lot of things might come to make you give up but hold on, that stumbling block shall become a stepping stone.

I have not said all I needed to say but I have said something, you might have started late but you can still be the latest. I pray for Guidance and direction from God for you, from today your steps shall be ordered by the lord. Be blessed.

You might be asking:

If truly God created me to be a solution to this world,
If truly God created me to be great;
If truly God created me to be the head and not the tail,
If truly God created me to be a light to this dark world;
If truly God created me to be a lender and not a borrower;

Why is my life like this?
Why am I finding it hard to eat?
Why am I not able to secure even an ordinary job?
Why is there no husband/wife to marry?

Why is my life full of struggle?
If the word of God is true, why is my life contrary to what God has said in His word?
The answers to your questions can be found in Matthew 13:24-28
"Another parable put He (Jesus) forth unto them, saying: The kingdom of heaven (what God has done) is likened unto a man which sowed good seed in his field. 25 But while men slept, his enemy came and sowed tares among the wheat, and went his way. 26 but when the blade was sprung up and brought forth fruit then appeared the tares, also. 27 so the servants of the householder came and said: Sir didst not thou sow good seed in thy field? From where, then hath the tares come from? 28 He said unto them: "An enemy (satan) hath done this…" (KJV)

The good seed, the bible is talking about here, are the good things which God has put in your life. In Genesis 1-2, it talked about how God created everything and He saw that, it was good.

Then God created a caretaker to take care of His creation. You and I are the care takers of this world.
A special assignment was given to you and I to be fruitful, multiply and to replenish the earth.
When God created your life, He saw that everything was good and perfect.

In God there is no imperfection.
Remember you are created in His image. It is the will of God for you to be fruitful. Fruitfulness is the kingdom of God, Good health is the kingdom of God. Prosperity is the kingdom of God. Salvation, peace, righteousness, love, joy and the Holy Ghost is the kingdom of God.
3 John: 2.

"Brethren, I wish above all things that thou prospereth and be in good health, even as thy soul prospereth" (KJV)

God`s desire is for us to enjoy our lives to the fullness. Remember in John 10:10b "….I came that you might have life and have it abundantly" When our life is filled with happiness, we will operate in the plan and purpose of God which He had in mind before He created us.

The tares which the bible is talking about here are the evil exchange which the enemy has done over your destiny. According to the scripture in Eccl. 10: 5-7; "There is an evil I have seen under the sun, 6- folly is set in great dignity, 7 - while the rich sit in a lowly place, I have seen servants on horses while princes walk on the ground like servants (NJKV). There are forces of darkness and they only operate in darkness. Their assignment is to change people's destinies. They are all over the place in our houses, offices, environments, families etc. There are wicked personalities using other people's destiny in order to prosper.

There was a story of deliverance programme in 2001. There was a sister that came to the deliverance programme, she looked like a zombie, saliva was gushing out of her mouth and a prayer point was called on a Monday,

"Any power using my virtue to prosper die, in the name of Jesus."

Then, on Wednesday, the news came that the elder brother of that sister who was a business man passed away. What happened is that, after her brother started his business, he went to the witch doctor for money making. He was asked to sleep with his sister in order to become rich. He succeeded to sleep with his sister and he started getting rich. But the more, he was getting rich, the more his sister was getting worse and worse. After the brother died, this sister started getting well.

Maybe, you are like that sister who ignorantly gave herself to sleep with her brother. Maybe, you have already given yourself to your brother, uncle, auntie, boyfriend, mother even your father to do one thing or the other to you in order to be rich and now you are struggling. I want you to understand that, you have sold your destiny. It is no longer with you. Your destiny is exchanged. You need to call upon God concerning your life and He will deliver you. Your greatest enemy is the power that does not want you to fulfil your destiny.

What are these powers doing?

They exchange your strength with weakness
They exchange your vision with frustration
They exchange your prayerfulness with prayerlessness
They can exchange your increase with decrease
They exchange progress with stagnancy
They exchange your confidence with inferiority:
When you don't have confidence; what will come up is inferiority.
Every opportunity you see is like you are not up to the task.
They can exchange your life with death: When I talk about death, it is not only physical death; but it can be financial death, martial death, academic death, health death, etc.
They exchange your light with darkness
They exchange your health with sickness
They can exchange someone's financial life with financial death
They can exchange your prosperity with poverty: were you rich and all of a sudden, your wealth begins to disappear?
They can exchange your vigilance with ignorance
They can exchange your wisdom with foolishness
They can exchange your hard work with laziness: Before you were doing very well but later on, you started slacking.
They can exchange your fulfilment with frustration
They can exchange your focus with distraction.

This is very much in use against the people by the devil. The devil is using it, to remove focus. The secret of success is to be focused. Because, if you look at the opposition, you will loose your divine position. Many people today failed because they allowed themselves to be distracted. The enemy will use distraction to remove people from their right track. Your vision will empower you to overcome the opposition. Your focus will help you to crush all the wiles of the devil that are militating against you. The path to success is very narrow but only few people used to walk in it. If you allow yourself to be distracted where you are supposed to fly high like an eagle, you will start crawling like a chicken. Opposition and distraction are parts of the journey but keep focused.
God told Abraham to look at the East, West, North and South and as far as he can see, he will possess it. If your destiny could not have been tampered with, you could not have been where you are today. You need to pray for God to restore your godly ordained destiny. If you want your life to change, you need to pray the kinds of prayers which others are not praying.

Stolen destiny
We must know that a person's destiny can be stolen. As a matter of fact, only few people manage to retain or control of their destiny. There are many destinies that have been aborted and left unfulfilled.
Adam, the first man created by God, is a perfect example of someone whose destiny was stolen. He was created to live in the glory of God in Eden and to lead other creatures in the worship of God. However, his glorious destiny or God's plan for his life was brought to an abrupt end because Adam yielded to Satan's deceit. Satan, the devil, stole Adam's destiny.
John 10:10;
"The thief cometh not, but for to steal, and to kill, and to destroy."

In our days, many people still wonder why they face tribulations and their lives have become the opposite of the life they desire to live.
Jeremiah 29:11;
While man was asleep, the enemy came to sew tares in the mist of the wheat".
Matthew 13:25.
This book is intended to assist everyone who must have lost track of his or her destiny to recover God's will for their.
As you read on or keep touch with this column, the promise of God in this regard as expressed in Joel 2:25-26 will be your portion in Jesus' name:
"And I will restore to you the years that the locust hath eaten, the cankerworm, and the caterpillar, and the palmerworm, my great army which I sent among you. And ye shall eat in plenty, and be satisfied, and praise the name of the LORD your God, that hath dealt wondrously with you: and my people shall never be ashamed."
Satan's targets
But you must watch; the devil usually targets three specific areas in the life of a believer, namely, one's spiritual power, position or throne and the believer's possessions.

The power base
God warned Adam that if he ate the fruit of the forbidden tree, he would lose his spiritual power: "Positive death". Satan, the devil, used deception to steal the power from Adam; so he died positively and his destiny was aborted.
Every believer whose attitude to prayer begins to decline, or is no longer as enthusiastic about Church programmes as he used to be, or faces the harassment of the devil in any department of his life and who is under serious pressure to succumb to the pressure of his Portipher's wife, should embark on a spiritual renewal and revival exercise

immediately so that the devil will not be able to steal his destiny.

HOW TO RECOVER YOUR STOLEN DESTINY

Your destiny is God's purpose and target for your life. It is always the prime target for Satan the devil, whose mission is to steal, destroy and kill.

Why do the enemy exchange destiny?
{Number 22:6, Exodus 1:8-16, Judges 16:5-6

Because the enemy wants to conquer him;
Because the enemy wants to suppress him;
Because the enemy wants to contend with his destiny;
Because his destiny is threatening the existence of another person;
Because his destiny is an eagle destiny;
Because he is trying to escape from the hands of a slave master;
Because somewhere somehow some persons, powers or personalities do not want to see him prosper;

You must safeguard your destiny.
Every man was created for a specific purpose. Destiny is God's life target for individuals. During creation, everyone was designed with certain abilities or capabilities to achieve a predetermined objective in God's system; and within a certain situation or circumstance of existence.
You did not come into existence by mere chance after all, especially looking at the biological formation of man. A single ejaculation from man during sexual intercourse produces 66 million spermatozoa; and only one sperm succeeds to fertilize the woman's egg, for a child to be formed.

The power that chooses the particular sperm that did the fertilization decides who results from the encounter. Your existence is indeed one against 66 million odds.
This proves that you are definitely a deliberate arrangement of God. The scripture bears eloquent testimonies to the fact of predestination
Jeremiah 1:5.
"Before I formed thee in the belly, I knew thee; and before thou camest forth out of the womb, I sanctified thee, and I ordained thee a prophet unto the nations".
Isaiah 49:1.
"Listen, O isles, unto me; and hearken, ye people, from far; The LORD hath called me from the womb; from the bowels of my mother hath he made mention of my name."
Romans 8:29;
"For whom he did foreknow, he also did predestinate to be conformed to the image of his Son, that he might be the firstborn among many brethren."

Your destiny shall be restore back to you whit entrees

The Ark of Covenant represents the presence of God in Israel. Any problem that the Ark of Covenant confronts vanished.
At the time Israel was to capture Jericho, River Jordan which they must cross in order to reach Jericho had overflown its banks. It was when the feet of the priest carrying the Ark touched the water of the river that God divided the water so that the people of Israel could cross on dry ground.

Because the Ark represented the power of the people of Israel, it became the prime target of the devil. The devil always targets the power of a believer. He causes a misunderstanding or suspicion between the believer and his spiritual master or prayer partner. He causes fatigue towards prayer. He does anything that weakens our prayer base for the purpose of dislocating our power.

Sin entered the land of Israel because Eli, the Priest and the Judge, was unable to control his two children from the misuse of the offering made to the Lord.
People of Philistines captured the Ark of Covenant and carried it straight into the house of their god, “Dagon”. It happens that the stolen destinies are given unto people who have no capacity to bear them. Same way Dagon fell before the Ark overnight. The Priest put the Dagon back into its position only to meet the dust of Dagon, the third day. It was completely dismembered because the power that was placed before it surpasses that which it could withstand. Same way, our destiny stolen, will crush those to whom they are given.
Ashdod was the city of Philistine that housed Dagon in whose shrine the Ark of Covenant was placed. The people of the city started to die in their thousands from pile and the tumor of the anus. They located the source of their problems as the Ark and requested the elders of Philistine to take it out of their domain.

The Ark of Covenant was taken to Gath and with the Ark, the torment of pile and tumor arrived in Gath. The people of Gath were dying in their thousands. They immediately requested the removal of the Ark to Ekron but the inhabitants of Ekron refused to have the Ark in their city. It really became a big problem for the Philistines. Same way, your destiny that was stolen will become a real problem to those that are holding it.

Upon spiritual consultation, the elders of Philistine were advised to return the Ark of Covenant to Israel. They were also told not to return only the Ark but a substantial Trespass Offering that must consist of gold made in the image of tumor. This is to demonstrate that they admitted to having overstepped their bounds and they were genuinely repentant. Of course, they quickly arranged the offering and set the Ark and the offering on a cart pulled by two animals which went straight to Israel.

Your power to prayer, gift of the Holy Spirit, hunger for the work of God, image and the likeness of God that the devil stole through his human agents will be returned to you with commission and interest.

THE PRICE REQUIRED TO BE PAID IN ORDER TO FULFILL GODS MASTER PLAN FOR YOUR LIFE

You must be born again; you must accept Jesus Christ as your personal Lord and savior. Paul had to accept Christ for His destiny to change. And you must get ready to walk diligently with God. Because you cannot determine your destiny you only discover it.

You must have the desire to find out what God has called you to do, and you can only find out by searching Gods word diligently.

You must be a reader of the right kind of books, Daniel said in Daniel chapter 2 vs. 9 that He understands by books. Paul too was a reader. All the great men that have caused drastic changes were readers so they became leaders, in this life you will rule in your respective field.

You must get the required the facts for your field; the book of proverbs says every enterprise is built by wise planning and getting the right facts. You must know the ingredients of music before you can be an effective musician.

You must search, yes search the right materials you are seeking to uncover as every valuable information opens up with a diligent, persistent search

Get wisdom and understanding, you must operate wisely, your destiny is great and glorious but there are phases and

chapters, so you must program and plan accordingly, what I mean is this, set short term and long term goals.
You must be spiritual, because spirituality is the booster of destiny, live a Holy, fraud free life, study the word, pray and fast so as to build enough capacity to defeat the oppositions because the enemy is envious of your destiny
You must value time, David said in psalms 90 vs 12; Oh lord teach us to number our days so that we can apply our heart to wisdom. You must live each day as if it is the last day so avoid procrastination.
You must be involved in charity in whatever level it gives you speed as you approach your desired goal. This also means you must think of others and not just yourself.
You must be proud of what you have been called to do, don't envy others
You must have mentors and role models in that same field you have chosen.

How can I escape from the Hands of Destiny Exchanger?
Repent from unknown and known sins;
Pray destiny restoring prayers;
Pray destiny rebuilding prayers;
Cancel all the evil transaction done against your destiny.

Prayer Points
Any power from my foundation, contesting over my destiny, die, in the name of Jesus.
Every destiny exchanger assigned to exchange my destiny catch fire, in the name of Jesus.
Thou destiny exchanger in my family line which has succeeded to exchange the destiny of my family members, my destiny is not your candidate, catch fire, in the name of Jesus.
Wherever my destiny has been caged, wherever the destinies of my children/spouse have been caged, I command you now to be released by fire, in t he name of Jesus.

Wherever my destiny has been hidden, I command you now to appear and locate me, in the name of Jesus.
I recover my destiny from the hand of destiny exchangers in the name of Jesus.
My destiny be released and locate me in the name of Jesus.
You the star of my destiny arise and shine, in the name of Jesus.
Every satanic transaction done over my life while I was in the womb, perish by the blood of Jesus, in the name of Jesus.
Anything stolen from my life while I was in the womb be restored by the blood of Jesus, in the name of Jesus.
Every serpent of darkness which has sucked my virtue, through sex with any satanic agent, vomit, my virtue and die, in the name of Jesus.
Every power from my foundation which has buried my family, my destiny is not your candidate, die, in the name of Jesus.
Thou ancient of Days, rebuke the devourer for my sake, in the name of Jesus.
Any personality that the devil has replaced my life with be roasted by fire, in the name of Jesus.
My exchanged destiny, be restored by the blood of Jesus, in the name of Jesus.
Any power assigned to exchange my destiny, die, in the name of Jesus
Every altar of the waster erected to waste my destiny, be roasted by fire in Jesus name.
Every pillar of witchcraft in the foundation of my life, crumble.
Any satanic strongman using the destinies of the family, to prosper, enough is enough, die in the name of Jesus.
I break myself loose from my national bondage, in the name of Jesus.
Every destiny quenchers sitting upon my destiny, be cast in the fire in the name of Jesus.

Every destiny destroyer sitting upon my destiny, be cast into the fire in the name of Jesus.

Any power sitting upon my life, blocking me from rising, be cast into the fire in the name of Jesus.

Every demonic attack, anywhere in this nation, erected to keep my destiny in the valley, by the thunder fire of God, shatter to pieces, in the name of Jesus.

Thank You Lord, in the name of Jesus.

BREAK UP YOUR FALLOW GROUND

Jeremiah 4:3. For thus saith the LORD to the men of Judah and Jerusalem, Break up your fallow ground, and sow not among thorns.

Hosea 10:12. Sow to yourselves in righteousness, reap in mercy; break up your fallow ground: for it is time to seek the LORD, till he come and rain righteousness upon you.

As a Christian before we can have our fallow ground broken there some steps for us to take.
Fallow ground is a field that has been sown with crops in the past and has yielded much fruit, but has now been left unworked for a time. It is hard and full of ruts. It yields nothing but weeds now. (There thousands believer today exhibiting the evil character of fallow ground like unbeliever) This is a picture of a land that used to be known for its righteousness but has now turned from God and grown cold toward Him. It is a perfect picture of society today that promote immorality on the Altar of the Lord. The verses leading up to verse twelve reveal the circumstances of the times.

Break we are saying is not to destroy but to cultivate or plant after cultivating you reap. It can also be to set or starts something.
It is time to break up old ways. It is time to put the sharp plow to the ground that is not bearing fruit. This is not an easy scripture because there is a moment where I must look with honesty at my heart… there are too many fallow areas there. I am busy and yet, I am not fertile. I have experienced barrenness in my life but I have forgotten what that looks like

in the heart. I believe it is time to look again… to accept the plow of God's Spirit.
"Sow for yourselves righteousness, reap in mercy; break up your fallow ground, for it is time to seek the Lord, till He comes and rains righteousness on you" Hosea 10:12
We read in 1 Peter 2:1-2, "Therefore laying aside all malice, all deceit, hypocrisy, envy, evil speaking,
As new-born baby you desire the sincere milk of the word, which you may grow thereby." Notice that when we lay aside the sins mentioned in verse one, we then become alive with the spiritual hunger and desire mentioned in verse two.
When we become content with where we are in God, and cease to pursue a deeper relationship with Him, we then have need of breaking up our fallow ground. As Hosea 10:12 states, when we break up our fallow ground we will find a fresh work of God in our lives, "till He comes and rains righteousness" on us as a result.

Fallow ground is untilled and uncultivated ground. It has been protected from the shock of the plow and the agitation of the farm equipment. Fallow ground lies undisturbed year after year. It remains the same, safe and unchanged. It never sees the fruit of the harvest season. And there is never a harvest without the plow first of all breaking up the hard, crusty soil.
On the other hand, cultivated, ploughed ground has allowed its peace and contentment with the ordinary to be disturbed by the plow. Ploughed ground experiences the travail of change. It has been upset, bruised, and broken. But it finds the rewards of the plow in the new life that it produces, and in the fruitful harvest.

Sow for yourselves righteousness, reap the fruit of unfailing love, and break up your unploughed ground; for it is time to seek the Lord, until he comes
and showers righteousness on you." (Hosea 10:12)

These passages have in common the phrase, "Break up your unploughed ground." Just what does it mean for me and you to do that?

The phrase "unploughed ground" (NIV) or "fallow ground" (KJV, NRSV) is the Hebrew noun nîr, "the tillable, untilled, or fallow ground."* It is land that could be productive, but for whatever reason has not been broken up, tilled, ploughed, and prepared for planting. The prophets speaking the Word of the Lord are commanding the people to break up that land -- spiritually! The prophets observe two things about fallow ground:

What It Means to break up the Fallow Ground

To break up the fallow ground, is to break up your hearts, to prepare your minds to bring forth fruit unto God. The mind of man is often compared to the ground in the bible. The word of God is the seed sown there, the fruit representing the actions and emotions of those who receive it. To break up the fallow ground therefore, is to bring the mind into such a state that it is fitted to receive the Word of God. Sometimes your hearts get matted down, hard and dry, until there is no such thing as getting fruit from them until they are broken up, and mellowed down, and fitted to the Word. It is this softening of the heart, so as to make it feel the truth, which the prophet calls break up your fallow ground.

John 7:38 He that believeth on me, as the scripture hath said, out of his belly shall flow rivers of living water

WHAT IS OUR FALLOW GROUND

Sin Heb.12:1
Wrong habitation (Eccl. 12:1)
Religion disguise (Matt. 5:20)
Desire to face men I send 31:4; II Sam.1:5-16
Impure life John 1:9

False security Sol. 31:1; ps.97:7
Self-righteousness Isaiah 64
Worldliness bad character John 4:4; II Tim.4:10; I Peter 2:24

THE BENEFIT OF BREAKING YOUR FALLOW GROUND

You are going to rap abundant harvest Matt. 13:8
You will make heaven by the end Ezekiel 33;1-8; Jer.4:1
The Cankerworm world be destroy Joel 2:25
The lost glory will be restored Ps. 126:6

In Conclusion: Remember necessity before us is that, if we don't bear fruit we shall be cut down. Matt.3:10, Rev. 22:1-22, Matt. 12:35.

CHANGE YOUR IDEAS TO BLESSING

In the book of Phil 4:13 'I can do all things through Christ which strengthens me'. The limitation should be broken will strength in thy Lord that anything you lay your hands shall prosper. Tell the limitation that you can do all things through Christ that strength you not few or small things, by this you will break up your fallow ground.

As a Christian, if you want anything just has that faith that it will be successful, do not limit yourself with the words of your mouth.

WHAT CAN HOLD YOU DOWN

FEAR OF MAN: 2 Tim.1:8 we should not be afraid of what men may do or say; just stretch forth and your aim(s) or goal(s) will be achieved. John 17:14-16, because you are not of the world they we surely hate you, just acknowledge that as you breaking up your enemies will not be at the same level again.

IMPURE LIFE: I John 1:9 "If we confess our sins, he is faithful and just to forgive us our sins, and to cleanse us from all unrighteousness". The bible says we should be careful of devil's devices, part of devices of devil is to make us no to forsake our sins and it will affect us from breaking our fallow ground. Heb. 12:1 "........ let us lay aside every weight, and the sin which doth so easily beset us, and let us run with patience the race that is set before us.

COMFORT: Christians who are found running after wealth will find themselves blamed; because Jesus has promised us that He supply all need our according to His riches in Glory by Christ Jesus. Our own is to be faithful to whatever business or job we do are doing. Our comfort will surely come. The book of I Tim.6:9-10 "But they tat will be rich fall into temptation and a snare......." Also Prov. 10:22 says "The blessing of the Lord, it make rich and he added no sorrow with". Jesus Christ comfort is everlasting comfort which added no sorrow. We need to recognize God in our situation and life.

INGORANCE: Sometime ignorance makes us not to break our fallow ground. In a situation where you have materials that will make you prosper but because you are ignorant of what is happening or how to use your resources, you find it difficult to break up your fallow ground. The Hosea 4:6 says "my people are destroyed for lack of knowledge, I will also reject thee..."

Some other points to consider are:
desire to please man I Sam. 31:4, I Sam. 1:5-6
Religious Activities Matthew 5:20
Covetousness Luke 12:5, Prov. 15:16
Power or Position Eccl. 2:9
Worldliness Jos. 4:4, I Tim. 4:10
Self-Righteousness Isa. 64:6

False Security Isa. 31:2, ps. 97:7

I am assuring you today that if you forsake this entire thing definitely you will break up your Fallow ground. Jesus Christ is faithful and just to forgive sins. He makes impossibilities possible. Rely solely on Him and He will not put you to shame.
Genesis 3:15

PRAYER POINTS:

Fire of God, heal my head now in the name of Jesus. (7 times)

I claim freedom from every evil pronouncement against my head.

Every force of affliction against my head disappear.

4. Blood of Jesus (7 hot times) repair my head now.
5. Every damage done to my head received permanent solution.
6. My head reject any evil manipulation.
7. Let every force of affliction be consumed by divine fire in the name of Jesus
8. All evil strangers come out of your hiding places in the name of Jesus
9. All bewitched properties receive deliverance in the name of Jesus
10. Let the handwriting of the enemy turn against him in the name of Jesus.
11. Let every evil king installed against me be paralyzed in the name of Jesus.
12. I paralyzed every satanic wrestler and struggler for my goodness in the name of Jesus.
13. Every stronghold of debt, be dashed to pieces in the name of Jesus.
14. Every stronghold of oppression, be dashed to pieces in the name of Jesus.

15. Every stronghold of loss, be dashed to pieces in the name of Jesus.
16. Let every hunter of my soul begin to shoot themselves in the name of Jesus.
17. Lord, empower my life with your anointing in the name of Jesus. (Place your right hand on your head)
18. Lord, let your healing power flow into my body in the name of Jesus
19. Lord, let your purging fire flow into my body in the name of Jesus.
20. Let my head be delivered from every pollution in the name of Jesus.
21. Lord, make the impossible possible for me in the name of Jesus.
22. O Lord, make a way for me where there is no way in the name of Jesus.
23. Every assignment and weapon of the enemy against me, be frustrated in the name of Jesus.
24. Every evil weapon fashioned against me be roasted in the name of Jesus
25. Every destiny destroyed by polygamy be reversed, in the name of Jesus.
26. Every witchcraft power working against my destiny, fall down and die, in the name of Jesus.
27. Every incantation and ritual working against my destiny, be disgraced, in the name of Jesus.
28. Every power of darkness assigned against my destiny, fall down and die, in the name of Jesus.
29. Every evil power trying to re-program my life, fall down and die, in the name of Jesus.
30. I reject every rearrangement of my destiny by household wickedness, in the name of Jesus.
31. Lord, anytime I want to make a mistake, direct me a right.
32. I refuse to be removed from the divine agenda, in the name of Jesus.

33. I refuse to be limited by any power of darkness, in the name of Jesus.
34. Every quencher of my destiny, fall down and die, in the name of Jesus.
35. O Lord, let my divine destiny appear and let perverted destiny disappear.
36. I reject every satanic re-arrangement of my destiny, in the name of Jesus.
37. I refuse to live below my divine standard, in Jesus' name.
38. Every evil power having negative awareness of my destiny, be impotent, in the name of Jesus.
39. I paralyze every destiny polluter, in the name of Jesus.
40. Let every door of attack on my spiritual progress be closed, in Jesus' name.
41. Holy Spirit set me on fire for God.
42. I command all my imprisoned benefits to be released, in Jesus' name.
43. The Lord should anoint me to pull down negative strongholds standing against me, in the name of Jesus.
44. Let the thunder fire of God strike down all demonic strongholds manufactured against me.
45. The Lord should anoint me with the power to pursue, overtake and recover my stolen properties from the enemy.

THERE IS A VACANCY FOR YOU UP THERE

(And you are the candidate for that throne)
Ex. 23:20-28, Proverb 18:16, Eccl.10:10-25, Psalm 110:2. Rev 4:1-2. Is. 22:20-23, Prov. 18:14-16. Gen. 27; 28-29
God's word for you this month is that ``there is a vacancy for you up there and not down here 'oh yes, you are the candidate for that position!" From today opposition will no more take your position. Every conspiracy in the higher places that wants to mortgage or transfer your birthright to another shall be overthrown. Rebecca, Esau's mother conspired and traded his birthright to Jacob that she loved, Genesis 27:1- 40. Mr Laban the father of sister Rachel used the law of seniority and gave the husband of Rachel to Leah, Gen. 29:21-29. From today any one toying with your glory shall be sacrificed for it like Harman.

After election campaigns there is always a selection, election and rejection even after all these were a group of people called divine candidates without campaign or election but just remembered for the next level. If you doubt ask Mephibosheth, II Samuel 9:1-13, or Joseph, Gen. 41:14-44, or David, 1 Samuel 16:1-14. You are the next to be lifted before 90 days from now.

Up there, there is a place where God has prepared for you. No matter how highly placed you are now, God still want you to be the best. If you are on higher ground or high place of authority, power, divine connection, favour, (everybody will always love to favour the person on top) you will control anything that surrounds you but in the valley many people lied down there. Higher place is where you belong. Much advantage is there for you:

Where you can see far
A place of defence
A place to get divine connection.
Land of opportunity
A place of fulfilment Ps.45:6-7
You will be the focus Prov.22:7 Prov.14:20

WHY MUST YOU GO UP?

JOHN LOST HIS HEAD TO A LITLE GIRL because he was not rightly positioned (anointing without money is annoyances, power without position is perilous, vision without provision is fluctuation) Matt.14:8.

Note: Many times, God's candidates for vacancies are unknown, immature, illiterates, unqualified. That is what is called unmerited favour, Acts 4:13.
Remember God called:
a runaway, murderer and a fugitive like Moses
a radical and an unschooled farmer like Elisa
an irrelevant, unsocial prisoner like Joseph
a scavenger and bastard like Japheth (Judges 11:1-8)
a cripple and forgotten like Mephibosheth
a persecutor, a terrorist and an activist like Saul of Tarsus
an ignorant and immature like Samuel to mention but a few.
So don't disqualify yourself, God never called the qualified but He qualifies the called.

God is looking at your direction today. He knows your past, present and future, and when He looks, He never see your failure but what He created you to be .i.e. when He saw the mad man of Gadarenes, He only saw a great evangelist in him. He could see divine treasure in Mary Magdalene and not a demonic or prostitute.

Higher ground means changing your position from where you are now to a higher place where there is no more struggle:

from barrenness to fruitfulness,
from poverty to wealth,
from sickness to good health.

To go higher, you need God because without God you can not go any farther in life. Then you need strength, energy, determination and effort. So determine to move forward. Some of us are ready to move higher but we still depend on our friends, family or sugar daddy. Ps.60:11, Mark 7:5-7, Jeremiah 17:1-8. Progress is good, Romans 8:31, Our God is the only one that has absolute power to take us to higher ground. Ps 121:1-2 James 1:17.

YOU MUST GET THERE BY:

Divine arrangement like King Saul
Divine Appointment like David
Divine connection like Elijah and Elisa
Divine favour like Mephibosheth
Divine enlargement like Peter, the fisherman

WHY MANY CAN'T OCCUPY THE HIGH PLACE?

Ignorance, Hosea 4;6
They believe it is too costly, Ps.139:6, Proverb 24:7
Activities of forces of darkness, Matt. 21:1-7
Lack of foresight, (What you see is what you will have)
Wrong desire, Lazarus Luke 16:21.
Looking for the living among the dead
Wrong location or association
Because of food (what will I eat) Gen. 25:29
Sin of the past, Gen. 35:22. Gen. 49:1-4
Partial obedience
Not ready to sacrifice

HOW TO MOVE TO HIGHER GROUND

Rededicate yourself to God, Genesis 35:1-
You must position yourself in the right place, Ruth 1:1-2
Let God be your partner in anything you are doing.

Humble yourself because pride is a killer.
Be a man of prayer (prayer may not change what you are passing through some times but it will change you or your position and the way you see things)
Have absolute faith and trust in the Lord, Isaiah 40:31
Holy Communion, I Kings 9:1-9
Learn how to praise God regularly

WHAT MUST I DO?

Forsake all for Christ sake (Abraham, Genesis12:1-. Elisha, I kings 19:15)
Now that you know that you are a special parson so preserved your body, spirit and soul for God, Roman 12:1-
Don't mind the opposition, in every Canaan there are children of ANAKI and before any throne is MR GOLIAT. Don't let what you are going through stop where you are going to!
Take your birthright
What does it take to be there Luke 2:40, Matt.3:17, Gal.4:1-2.
Working with God, Genesis 17:1, Psalm 24:7, Romans 8:31, Isaiah 51:1, Genesis 5:24, II Chron. 15:2.
Agree with God, Amos 3:3, and obey Him, Isaiah 1:19.
Move from where you are, Deut.2:3, Proverb. 4:18.
Ready to take a risk
Ask for Anointing for Divine Grace to get there.
I WILL SEE YOU ON TOP!

Gen 38:19-20. Gen 38:19. 2 Sam 20:3. Isa 47:9. Isa 54:4. 2 Sam 20:3-7. Isa 47:9-12.
Isa 54:4-6. 1 Kings 17:12-24. 1 Kings 18:1-8

Breaking the limitation and get the tangible achievement, no more failure at the edge of success or almost there but never be there, rise up to take up your destiny, don't die as a tenant, servant, employee, Berger. You can make it. I refuse to end as a failure.

1 Samuel 17

Confessions: Numbers 23:23: “Surely there is no enchantment against Jacob, neither is there any divination against Israel: according to this time it shall be said of Jacob and of Israel, What hath God wrought!”

1. Earth, earth, earth, hear the word of the Lord, swallow every enchanter assigned against me, in the name of Jesus.
2. Crystal balls of the enemy explode in their faces, in the name of Jesus.
3. Any power calling for my head before evil mirrors, die with the mirror, in the name of Jesus.
4. Herod of my father’s house, go back to the Red Sea, in the name of Jesus.
5. Messenger of frustration, carry your message back to your sender, in the name of Jesus.
6. Messenger of affliction, release your affliction on your sender, in the name of Jesus.
7. Problems caused by enchantment, pack your load and go, in the name of Jesus.
8. Every chain limiting my favor, break, in the name of Jesus.
9. Infirmity, fall away from my life, in the name of Jesus.
10. Every bondage against my brain, break, in the name of Jesus.
11. I break the law of death over my life, in the name of Jesus.
12. Every consultation of sorcerers against me, be scattered, in the name of Jesus.
13. Every power harboring enchantments against me, die, in the name of Jesus.
14. Sun, moon and stars, vomit every enchantment against my life, in the name of Jesus.

15. Enchantments, you will not settle down in my life, in the name of Jesus.
16. Every magic poured on the ground to subdue my life, backfire, in the name of Jesus.
17. Every power that weakens my spiritual authority, die, in the name of Jesus.
18. Masquerades assigned to sleep in my house, die, in the name of Jesus.
19. O sun, arise, smite everything assigned against me, in the name of Jesus.
20. My Father, whatsoever you have not planted in my life, uproot them, in the name of Jesus.
21. My Father, appear in my situation by fire, in the name of Jesus.
22. Dead bones of my life, rise up from the dead, in the name of Jesus.
23. My star, manifest by fire, in the name of Jesus.
24. Power of God, arise, and bulldoze my way unto breakthroughs, in the name of Jesus.
25. Every evil spiritual umbilical cord through which poison flows into my destiny, catch fire.
26. Evil prayer mats assigned against me, die, in the name of Jesus.
27. Dry bones of my destiny, come alive, in the name of Jesus.
28. Every power assigned to terminate my purpose on earth, die, in the name of Jesus.
29. Every power that wants me to die undiscovered, die, in the name of Jesus.
30. Every power that wants me to die unused, die, in the name of Jesus.
31. Every power that wants me to die uncelebrated, die, in the name of Jesus.
32. Every power that wants me to die unaccomplished, die, in the name of Jesus.

33. Every power that wants me to die unfulfilled, die, in the name of Jesus.
34. Strange forces holding me down, let me go, in the name of Jesus.
35. Every rope tying me down to the same spot, break, in the name of Jesus.
36. Curses, barriers of limitation, die, in the name of Jesus.

ARISE SHINE

"Arise, Shine, for thy light is come, and the glory of the Lord is upon thee" Isa. 60:1
For someone to arise, it shows that such a person has been sleeping or sitting down-doing nothing. Wherefore he saith, "Awake thou that slept and arise from the dead, and Christ shall give thee light". Eph. 5:14, For too long we have been sleeping, not living a fulfilled life, whereas the Lord says, we are light of the World (Math. 5:14, I Thess. 5:5-7) let us not sleep as others do, but let us watch and be sober.

There is darkness in the world "For, behold, the darkness shall cover the earth, and gross darkness the people, but the LORD shall rise upon thee, and HIS glory shall be seen upon thee Isa. 60:2 "You are so important to God, God is coming on you. At creation, the bible tells us that the earth was without form and void and the spirit of the Lord was upon the face of the deep and God said, "Let there be light and there was light", Gen. 1:1-3. From that moment, creation became meaningful; I hope you are going to disappoint God who cares so much for you.

WHAT IS DARKNESS?

1. When there is loss of vision –Micah 3:6 "Now the night will close around you, cutting off all your visions. Darkness will cover you, making it impossible for you to predict the future. The sun will set for you prophets, and your day will come to an end." Because of loss of vision, today many are saying, "thus says the Lord", when God has actually said nothing".

2. When there is no enlightenment "And this is the condemnation, that light is come into the world and men loved darkness rather than light, because their deeds were evil, John 3:19". "They know not, neither will they understood, they walk in darkness all the foundation of the earth of the heart are not of course, Ps. 82:5".

Blindness, dullness and hardness of the heart make it impossible to see and understand the mind of God. "The way of the wicked is as darkness, they know not of what they stumble, Prov. 4:19".

THE USEFULNESS OF LIGHT

1. It gives light – Making clear the way "neither do men light a candle and put it under a bushel, but on a candlestick, and it gives light unto the entire house. Matt.5:16 "God expects you to give light to everyone around you.

2. It makes people see – "Let your light so shine before men, that they may see your good works, and glorify your father which is in heaven Matthew 5:16, "By letting people see your good work you make them see the glory of God through you, which will bring joy to His heart.

3. It lightens our path "Thy word is a lamp unto my feet and a light unto my path Ps. 119:105, "By being light, you will

prevent many people from failing into the pit of this world and even from going astray from the lord their maker

Let us arise, therefore, and show the light of the gospel of our lord Jesus Christ unto others. "The night is far spent, the day is at hand, let us therefore cast all the work of darkness and let us put on the whole armour of light. Let us walk honestly as in the day not in rioting and drunkenness, not in chambering and wantonness, not in strife and envying. But put ye on the Lord Jesus Christ and make not provision for the flesh to fulfill the lusts thereof. Rom.13:12-14 "For yes were sometimes darkness now are ye light in the Lord; walk as children of light" Eph. 5:8.

Let us therefore obey the great commission – "Go ye therefore and teach all nations baptizing them in the name of the Father and of the Son and of the Holy Ghost. Teaching to observe all things I have commanded you: and, lo, I am with you always, even unto the end of the world. Amen

Matthew 28:19-20.
Certainly, we are not left alone; in obeying the command. The Lord himself had promised being with us, our success is guaranteed. Jesus Christ is the light of the world. "In Him was life, and the life was the light of men" Jn.1:4 "For God who commanded the light to shine out of darkness, hath shine in our hearts, to give the light of the knowledge of the glory of God in the face of Jesus Christ" II Cor. 4:6.

Failure to do it will make us unprofitable servants. I pray that this will never be our portion in Jesus name. Amen.

Let us go therefore in the strength of the Lord of Host who goeth before His army He has promised He will be with us always Matt. 28:20.

ADVANTAGES

1. You will be wise – "The fruit of the righteous is a tree of life and he that winneth souls is wise" Prov. 11:30.
2. You will shine as brightness of the firmament. "And they that be wise shall shine as the brightness, and they that turn many to righteousness as the stars for ever and ever". Dan.12:3.
3. There is crown of glory awaiting us "And when the chief shepherd shall appear, ye shall receive the crown of glory that fadeth not away". I Peter 5:4.

Let us be diligent therefore and shine, for God is a rewarder of them that diligently seek Him. Heb. 11:6. Therefore my beloved brethren be ye steadfast, unmovable, always abounding in the work of the Lord, for as much as ye know that your labour is not in vain in the Lord". I Cor. 15:58.

But if you have not given your life to Jesus, I tell you, you are not yet of his own. And it will not be possible for you to rise and shine. Therefore, as you are reading this, surrender and yield your life to Jesus. He loves you, He died for you. He wants to enlist you in His army. If you are willing and obedient, you will eat the good of the land (Isa.1:19. "Behold, I stand at the door, and knock, I will come in to him, and I will live with him and he with me. "Rev.3:20".

Please don't keep Jesus outside any longer. Let Him come into your heart today and be born again; and have testimonies of His goodness and blessings.

Arise and shine and the glory of the LORD shall be upon thee. God bless you.

Ex. 11: 4 -7, Deut 23: 18, Psalm 22:16-20, Rev. 22:15

1. Let every dog barking against my progress, be paralyzed, in the name of Jesus.

2. I cancel every dream of spiritual failure, in the name of Jesus.
3. Every evil thing uttered against me by the tongue of the dead, be cancelled by the blood of Jesus.
4. Let the tongue of my oppressors be confused, in the name of Jesus.
5. Let my miracle cause revival in my family, in the mighty name of Jesus.
6. By the power that is in the blood of Jesus, I close every satanic door, in the name of Jesus.
7. I refuse to be used as satanic experiment, in Jesus' name.
8. I ask for angelic assistance to paralyze every satanic army directed against my home, in Jesus' name.
9. Every water spirit operating against me, receive the thunder of God, in Jesus' name.
10. I break every demonic crown upon my head, in the name of Jesus.
11. Let the fire and thunder of God attack all the powers of witchcraft working against me, in the mighty name of Jesus.
12. Every agent of the devil sent from the bottom of hell fire, receive madness, in the name of Jesus.
13. Every herbalist working on my name, be frustrated, in the name of Jesus.
14. Every satanic prayer uttered against me, go back to your sender, in the name of Jesus.
15. I refuse to reap any satanic harvest, in the name of Jesus.
16. You devil, hear me and hear me well, you cannot steal my blessings anymore, in the name of Jesus.
17. Father Lord, I thank you for answers to my prayers, in the name of Jesus.

COMING OUT AND GOING IN

Anyone who stops dreaming,
Has become one of the living dead
Don't let this happen to you
Be part of the opposition called 'life'!
Change your existence by daring
Dare!!!
Dare to live out your dreams to the full

“Do Not Give The Devil A Foothold” Ephesians 2:27

Before God’s people could get out of Egypt. Pharaoh made then three different offers. To each Moses said, “No “otherwise they’d never have got out. First, Pharaoh said, “Go only leave your children here”. Next, he said “Go only leave your business here”. Finally he said, “Go only don’t go too far”. Listen to what Moses told him. “There shall…Not a hoof can be left behind…” (Ex.10:26).

That's what you've got to do too – look the enemy in the eye and say, "No I'm taking my family, I'm taking my business and I'm going all the way with God! That's what it takes to get out of Egypt!

But what about getting into the Promised Land? This happened only one city as a time. One habit at a time…one attribute at a time….one step of faith at a time.

It happens when you break the enemy's hold on your finances and put God first. It happens when you take the remote control out of his hand and protect your family from an entertainment culture that corrupts. It happens when you refuse to contradict what God has said about you in His Word. Never speak words that make you refuse to contradict what God has said about you in His Word. Never speak words that make the enemy think he's still in control – he's now! The Bible says you have authority to drive him out – and he's got to go (Lk. 10:17). If you allow him even an inch, he'll turn it into a stronghold.

Rise up in faith today and announce I'm coming out and I'm going in!

PRAYERS FOR SPIRITUAL SANITATION

2 TIM. 2.21: If any man therefore purge himself from these, he shall be a vessel unto honor, sanctified and meet for the master's use and prepared unto every good work.

PRAYER POINTS:

I release myself from every ancestral demonic pollution in the name of Jesus.

I release myself from every demonic pollution emanating from my parent's religion in the name of Jesus.

3. I release myself from every demonic pollution

emanating from my past involvement in any demonic religion in the name of Jesus.

4. I break and loose myself from every idol and related associations in the name of Jesus.
5. I release myself from every dream pollution in the name of Jesus.
6. Let every satanic attack against my life in my dreams be converted to victory in the name of Jesus.
7. Let all rivers, trees, forests, evil companions, evil pursuers, visions of dead relative, snakes, spirit husbands, spirit wives and masquerades manipulated against me in the dream be completely destroyed by the power in the blood of Jesus.
8. I command every evil plantation in my life to come out all roots in the name of Jesus. (Lay your hands on your stomach and keep repeating the emphasized area).
9. All evil strangers in my body come out of your hiding places in the name of Jesus.
10. I disconnect any conscious and unconscious linkage with demonic caterers in the name of Jesus.
11. Let all avenues of eating and drinking spiritual poisons be closed in the name of Jesus.
12. I cough out and vomit any food eaten from the table of the devil in the name of Jesus. (Cough and vomit them out by faith, Prime the expulsion.)
13. Let all negative material circulating in my blood stream be evacuated in the name of Jesus.
14. I drink the blood of Jesus. (Physically swallow and drink it in faith. Do this for some time).
15. Lay one hand on your head and the other on your stomach or navel and begin to pray like this: Holy Ghost fire, burn from the top of my head to the sole of my feet. Begin to mention every organ in your body: kidney, blood, hearth, intestines, etc. Do not rush because the fire will actually burn.

16. I cut myself off from every spirit . . . . (Mention the name of your place of birth/origin) in the name of Jesus.
17. I cut myself off from every tribal spirit and curses in the name of Jesus.
18. I cut myself off from every territorial spirit and curse in the name of Jesus.
19. Holy Ghost purge my life in the name of Jesus.
20. I claim my complete deliverance from the spirit of ...... (Mention those things that you do not desire in your life) in the name of Jesus.
21. I break the hold of any evil power over my life in the name of Jesus.
22. Thank God for answers to your prayers.

MYSTERY OF LOCATION

Your location determine your allocation, success, fruitfulness, vision, accessibility, connection

Matthew 21:1-4. And when they drew nigh unto Jerusalem, and were come to Bethphage, unto the mount of Olives, then sent Jesus two disciples,
Saying unto them, Go into the village over against you, and straightway ye shall find an ass tied, and a colt with her: loose them, and bring them unto me.
And if any man say ought unto you, ye shall say, The Lord hath need of them; and straightway he will send them.
All this was done, that it might be fulfilled which was spoken by the prophet, saying,

2 Kings 2:19-22
And the men of the city said unto Elisha, Behold, I pray thee, the situation of this city is pleasant, as my lord seeth: but the water is naught, and the ground barren.
And he said, Bring me a new cruse, and put salt therein. And they brought it to him.
And he went forth unto the spring of the waters, and cast the salt in there, and said, Thus saith the LORD, I have healed

these waters; there shall not be from thence any more death or barren land.
So the waters were healed unto this day, according to the saying of Elisha which he spake.

II King 2:19-21, 8:1-6, Gen. 22:1-4, 26:1-3, Number 13:26-33

Dan 10:10-11:1
And, behold, an hand touched me, which set me upon my knees and upon the palms of my hands.
And he said unto me, O Daniel, a man greatly beloved, understand the words that I speak unto thee, and stand upright: for unto thee am I now sent. And when he had spoken this word unto me, I stood trembling.
Then said he unto me, Fear not, Daniel: for from the first day that thou didst set thine heart to understand, and to chasten thyself before thy God, thy words were heard, and I am come for thy words.

But the prince of the kingdom of Persia withstood me one and twenty days: but, lo, Michael, one of the chief princes, came to help me; and I remained there with the kings of Persia.
Now I am come to make thee understand what shall befall thy people in the latter days: for yet the vision is for many days.
And when he had spoken such words unto me, I set my face toward the ground, and I became dumb.
And, behold, one like the similitude of the sons of men touched my lips: then I opened my mouth, and spake, and said unto him that stood before me, O my lord, by the vision my sorrows are turned upon me, and I have retained no strength.

For how can the servant of this my lord talk with this my lord? for as for me, straightway there remained no strength in me, neither is there breath left in me.
Then there came again and touched me one like the appearance of a man, and he strengthened me,
And said, O man greatly beloved, fear not: peace be unto thee, be strong, yea, be strong. And when he had spoken unto me, I was strengthened, and said, Let my lord speak; for thou hast strengthened me.

Then said he, Knowest thou wherefore I come unto thee? and now will I return to fight with the prince of Persia: and when I am gone forth, lo, the prince of Grecia shall come.
But I will shew thee that which is noted in the scripture of truth: and there is none that holdeth with me in these things, but Michael your prince.

Mark 8:22-26
And he cometh to Bethsaida; and they bring a blind man unto him, and besought him to touch him.
And he took the blind man by the hand, and led him out of the town; and when he had spit on his eyes, and put his hands upon him, he asked him if he saw ought.
And he looked up, and said, I see men as trees, walking.
After that he put his hands again upon his eyes, and made him look up: and he was restored, and saw every man clearly.
And he sent him away to his house, saying, Neither go into the town, nor tell it to any in the town.

Not every location can favour all people that are why God instructed people like Abraham, Jacob, Joseph the parents of Jesus to relocate.
In the mark 8:22-22. You can see that Jesus dragged the man out of the town before any miracle can take place.
Because the town is under curse {Matthew 11:20-24}

It is that same town that fish swallow Jesus tax money, (marine power)
Until Jesus angrily told peter to arrest them with hock to recover their allocation money

Your location will determine your allocation and association

Isa 45:1-3
Thus saith the LORD to his anointed, to Cyrus, whose right hand I have holden, to subdue nations before him; and I will loose the loins of kings, to open before him the two leaved gates; and the gates shall not be shut;
I will go before thee, and make the crooked places straight: I will break in pieces the gates of brass, and cut in sunder the bars of iron:
And I will give thee the treasures of darkness, and hidden riches of secret places, that thou mayest know that I, the LORD, which call thee by thy name, am the God of Israel. KJV

Gen 29:1-3
Then Jacob went on his journey, and came into the land of the people of the east.
And he looked, and behold a well in the field, and, lo, there were three flocks of sheep lying by it; for out of that well they watered the flocks: and a great stone was upon the well's mouth.
And thither were all the flocks gathered: and they rolled the stone from the well's mouth, and watered the sheep, and put the stone again upon the well's mouth in his place.
Look a t this few point

loose the loins of kings, to open before him the two leaved gates. (evil decree from authority that close my door must be revised)

crooked places straight. (every bad news that pollute my personality must be rewrite)
break in pieces the gates of brass. (every invisible gate in my location that hinder my allocation crumble)
Cut in sunder the bars of iron. (every evil bar that limit me to minimum that enemy have erected in my location that never let big miracle access but only small break by fire)
Treasures of darkness, and hidden riches of secret places. (that hidden blessing and impression miracle be released today)

Land of the people of the east.(as I face the east my shadow{problem} must be behind me from today}
Looked, and behold a well in the field. {o lord open my eye to see the cover well of prosperity in my location}
Three flocks of sheep lying by it. {everyone is expecting to drink from my well}
great stone was upon the well's mouth.{who cover my glory today I receive the key to uncover it}
and they rolled the stone from the well's mouth, and watered the sheep

Acts 8:5-25

Then Philip went down to the city of Samaria, and preached Christ unto them.
And the people with one accord gave heed unto those things which Philip spake, hearing and seeing the miracles which he did.
For unclean spirits, crying with loud voice, came out of many that were possessed with them: and many taken with palsies, and that were lame, were healed.
And there was great joy in that city.
But there was a certain man, called Simon, which before time in the same city used sorcery, and bewitched the people of Samaria, giving out that himself was some great one:

To whom they all gave heed, from the least to the greatest, saying, This man is the great power of God.
And to him they had regard, because that of long time he had bewitched them with sorceries.

But when they believed Philip preaching the things concerning the kingdom of God, and the name of Jesus Christ, they were baptized, both men and women.
Then Simon himself believed also: and when he was baptized, he continued with Philip, and wondered, beholding the miracles and signs which were done.
Now when the apostles which were at Jerusalem heard that Samaria had received the word of God, they sent unto them Peter and John:
Who, when they were come down, prayed for them, that they might receive the Holy Ghost:
For as yet he was fallen upon none of them: only they were baptized in the name of the Lord Jesus.)
Then laid they their hands on them, and they received the Holy Ghost.

And when Simon saw that through laying on of the apostles' hands the Holy Ghost was given, he offered them money,
Saying, Give me also this power, that on whomsoever I lay hands, he may receive the Holy Ghost.
But Peter said unto him, Thy money perish with thee, because thou hast thought that the gift of God may be purchased with money.
Thou hast neither part nor lot in this matter: for thy heart is not right in the sight of God.
Repent therefore of this thy wickedness, and pray God, if perhaps the thought of thine heart may be forgiven thee.
For I perceive that thou art in the gall of bitterness, and in the bond of iniquity.

Then answered Simon, and said, Pray ye to the Lord for me, that none of these things which ye have spoken come upon me.

Dealing with Sorcery in the Land

There was sickness in the land, but it never bothered them. Unclean spirits were everywhere, almost in everyone, yet they felt strangely normal and 'happy,' or at least satisfied. A blanket of sadness was over all, yet they still believed that Simon was the answer to all their problems, whereas he was the very question and the very problem himself. Slowly they were dying, but ironically, dying happily, singing "Hosanna" to the very one drowning their boat. It was not a normal condition. It was the effect of sorcery over Samaria.

1 king 16:34.

Every unbroken cures over your location will not be fulfill over you and your family.

There are several locations in life that is why people are moving from one location to another. Different seeds fell at different location. Every location has a time of allocation. Every location needs personality before activation. In every location, there is allocation either good or bad and in every position there is always an opposition. Among the friend and foe there is always a covenant that birth to every location and the name given to them e.g.

1.Gaza

2. Gel boa I Sam.1:21

3.Bethsaida Mark 8:22, 11:21

4. Jericho Joshua6:26, I king 16:34, II King 2:19 5. Jordan

Every child of destiny has a specific route of destination that will lead them to their destiny and there are some important locations where God have predestined them to be at a specific time or at the appointed time.

DOMINATING YOUR DOMAIN

1kings 17:1 and Elijah the Tishbite, who was of the inhabitants of Gilead….Elijah only lived in Gilead but he was not a citizen of Gilead and his finances, health and destiny was not controlled by the forces of Gilead, just like you. You are in Nigeria but not controlled by the situation of Niger, your allocation and resources are from heaven because you are a citizen of heaven, a resident on earth and by location Nigeria.

Where you are not what you are, so don't let your enemy define your life by where you are now or your experience at the moment because god is taking you to a greater level.
You are in the world but not of the world. Sent to the world but not sent by the world. You are in charge to take charge not on an errand. You are to stand out but not to blend in.

Luke 3:16, Jer 20:9, Ps 39:3, Job 32:18-20, Acts 2:1-4

1. Thank God for the purifying power of the fire of the Holy Ghost.
2. I cover myself with the blood of the Lord Jesus.
3. Father let your fire that burns away every deposit of the enemy fall upon me, in the name of Jesus.
4. Holy Ghost fire incubate me, in the name of the Lord Jesus Christ.
5. I reject any evil stamp or seal placed upon me by ancestral spirits, in the name of Jesus.
6. I release any evil stamp or seal placed upon me by ancestral spirits, in the name of Jesus.
7. Let every door of spiritual leakage be roasted, in the name of Jesus.
8. I challenge every organ of my body with the fire of the Holy Spirit. (Lay your right hand methodically on various parts of the body beginning from the head)

9. Let every human spirit attacking my own spirit release me, in the might name of Jesus.
10. I reject every spirit of the tail, in the name of Jesus.
11. Sing this song: Holy Ghost fire, fire fall on me.
12. Let all evil marks be burnt off by the fire of the Holy spirit in the name of Jesus.
13. Let the anointing of the Holy Ghost fall upon me and break every negative yoke, in the name of Jesus.
14. Let every garment of hindrance and dirtiness be dissolved by the fire of the Holy Ghost, in the name of Jesus.
15. I command all my chained blessings to be unchained, in the name of Jesus.
16. Let all spiritual cages inhibiting my progress be roasted by the fire of the Holy Spirit, in the name of Jesus.

DIVINE HELP

1 Samuel 7:12. Ps 118:13. 1saiah 49;8, rev 12;16, Hebrew 4;16, Act 26;22, 16;9, Psalm 121;2, 124;8, 94;17, 71;12 25;1-2

MY HELPER must locate me, remember me, recognize me, help me, not become my tormentors and not fight me. What is help? Who needs help? Who can help and when you lack helpers, what happens?
After creation God discovered only one lack in man's life, that is inability to survive without help or helper, and God made helpmate for him.
Help have several names; Mercy, favour, grace, assistance, empowerment, encouragement, grant, gift, arms, support, care, direction, protection. Etc.

DIVINE HELP COMES THROUGH FAVOUR FROM OTHERS,YOUR LEADER AS A LADDER OR YOUR PARTNER?

YOU MUST BE FAVOURED.
"All men are equal until favour separates them into classes"

Favour is divine partiality. It is when God prefers you above others. Jacob was favoured; the Lord said; Jacob have I loved, Esau have I hated. Without God's favour, the labour of man will be fruitless. The difference between where you are and where you need to be is favour. The difference between those who fail and those who succeed is favour. There are two classes of people on earth: those who make it and those who miss it and the difference is favour.

Favour turns a nonentity into a celebrity, ridicule into a miracle, a back bencher into a front-liner. To increase in stature without increase in favour is a liability. For without favour, man will be a failure. Favour makes a man distinct. In a situation where people are doing the same thing but getting different results, it's favour that makes the difference. Get God's backing and pray to Him to make you a candidate of favour. Have you attended a very competitive interview before? You get to discover that the high and the mighty have their candidates therein.

Everyone that made it in the Bible went through the channel of favour. When you click on the favour button, where there is no way, a way is made for you.

You would not have heard about Joseph if favour was not on his side. The opposition against him was frightening but favour catapulted him to where he was destined to be.

Favour is a label, which when God wears on you everywhere you appear, you will be identified and assisted. He who wears favour cannot be missing in the crowd. That will be your portion in Jesus name.

"YOU NEED A LEADER AS A LADDER".

And he said to them "Follow me, and I will make you fishers of men".

Mathew 4:19.

There are people that put in all they have into what they believe in, yet things are not working for them as they desired, for those in this category, there must be some fundamental problems responsible for their predicaments. Life is based on principle. One of the principles is having a leader that can be used as a ladder to move up. You need a mentor to reach the top; you need a father to go further and a master to matter.

Instead of wasting away, why not identify heroes in your field: ministry, politics, business, academics, industry etc. There is nothing you wish to become that some people have not already become. Identify one or at most two of such people and be close to them.

Establish a father-son or mother-daughter relationship with your hero or heroine. Make him or her your mentor, call him or her father or mother. Never be ashamed, afraid or too proud to be a son to someone. If you do not have a hero, you may end up a zero.

WHO IS YOUR PARTNER?

The person you are travelling with determines what gets across to you"

"Iron sharpens iron, and one man sharpens another". Proverbs 27:17

Those that are not adding to you will definitely be removing from you, so be careful how you balance your relationship with them.

WHO NEED DIVINE HELP?

Proverbs 3:5-6.

"If what you have to accomplish is not bigger than you, then you do not need God"

Those that have been disappointed by men.

Those that want to accomplish more than their ability.

Those that have been pushed to the wall.

When our challenges are more than what we can handle by human strength.

Examples
John 5:7. Lack of help led to 38 years of sickness.
If not for a helper called Joseph of Arimathaea, Jesus' body would not have been given proper burial. May you locate yours today.
For Joshua to overcome Jericho, God had to send help from heaven to show the secret of victory to him.
David became great because of unusual help. 1chroncles 12:21-22.
Destiny without helpers will die as a slave in the land of his dominion
Celebrity without helpers will be frustrated.
An Anointed without helpers will lose his anointing in the wilderness of struggle.

You were born naked to proof that you need help, God knew the family that gave birth to Jesus as a very poor one so He sent three helpers to them in the name of wise men, that blessed them with gold frankincense and myrrh.
The Widow of the prophet almost lost her two sons like her husband if not for Elisha's help.
If not for divine help through Pharaoh's cup bearer, Joseph dream of the throne would have ended in the pit.
Esther would never have become a queen if Mordecai had not nurtured her.
Hosea 12:13. Destinies were preserved by the prophet. 2chroncles 24:1-2. Joash became king at the age of 7. And succeed because he was helped by his pastor as he obeyed him. Etc.

WHAT ARE THE SIGNS OF HELPLESSNESS
Being Stranded
Hopelessness

Nakedness

why many miss their helper

Many miss their helpers because they disguise as an enemy or someone that needs their help. We can see from the Bible that God first asked those He eventually helped for help. e.g. Widow of Zarephath, Shunamite woman, Peter that caught no fish, the woman at Jacob's well, Abraham, the boy with 5loaves and two fishes, Isaac before he blessed his son, etc. if you fail to help even in that position of need and lack, you will miss your helper. Psalm 126:1-6.

Proverb 29:15.When you take it personal anytime you're corrected claiming you are no longer a baby. When you refuse to fulfil your financial commitments, believing that making such sacrifices is to enrich your pastor or church. Deuteronomy 32:15-17. Psalm 119:67.

Have you discovered why many never help you before now?

Many in life are shadow chasers because they cannot locate the root of their problems. Do not take the symptoms for the sickness; every problem has roots. Symptoms are mere fruits and only root gives birth to fruits. If you merely pluck the fruits from a tree, you have not affected the tree in anyway as it will bear same type of fruits again. If you are able to dig to the tap root of the tree and cut it then the stem, the branches and the fruits will dry up. Stop giving your problem a symptomatic treatment, get to the root. Identify and understand your problem, for that is where progress begins.

Trace that problem to the specific root. For instance, the problems that often plague marriages are traceable to the wrong foundations laid for such earlier in life. Indeed, many married in ignorance. Marriage should be between two friends but when two strangers tied the nuptial knots, there will be problems.

Your deteriorating health may be a result of eating the wrong food or due to stress. The root of your problem may be certain things from your background, some wrong persons or habits that you have allowed to gain access into your life. Many problems also have spiritual roots but majority are not as spiritual as the traditional, cultural and superstitious beliefs portray them.

Locate your problem; trace it to the root and look for the way out. There is no situation that has no solution; once the root is identified, the solution will become obvious. Then start working things out; it might involve a painful decision, sacrifice, self-discipline or a re-orientation, but whatever it takes, do it to be free.

DIVINE HELP "Heaven helps those who cannot help themselves"

"For as the body without the spirit is dead, so faith without work is dead also".

James 2:26

Heaven is always there to help and does not discriminate against anyone. God cannot help you than you are willing to help yourself. Until you take steps in the direction of your expectation, those sent to help you will not emerge. It is the step you take that provokes the help you get. Psalms 37:23 says; "The steps of the righteous are ordered by God". I then add that only the righteous that takes step will have his/her steps ordered.

Many are waiting patiently till God will do it for them. Such people will wait forever for one must take the lead for God to supply the help. Know that nothing moves until you move.

Establish yourself today. No matter how small, make sure you start as long as you know what you want to achieve. No one is ready to support ideas that are not expressed; you must write your vision this 2013. If you want people to run along with you. Put all you have in your dream for it is your attitude that will determine the type of people that will be attracted to you. As long as your attitude is right; help will come.

As you establish yourself and work tirelessly on your assignment, heaven will open up to you. 2013 is the year you have been waiting for. Divine help will locate you in Jesus name.

PURSUE, OVERTAKE AND RECOVER

1 Sam. 30 . Psalm 18:37

PRAYER POINTS:

1. Thank God for His love, and mercy on you.
2. Praise the Lord with this chorus: "Who is like unto Thee . . .?"
3. The Lord should ordain terrifying noises unto the camp of the enemies of the gospel in my life (II Kings 7:6,7).
4. I command every satanic embargo on my goodness and prosperity to be scattered to irreparable pieces, in the name of Jesus.
5. Let every door of attack on my spiritual progress be closed, in Jesus' name.
6. Holy Spirit, set me on Fire for God.
7. I command all my imprisoned benefits to be released, in Jesus' name.
8. The Lord should anoint me to pull down negative strongholds standing against me, in the name of Jesus.
9. Let the thunder fire of God strike down all demonic strongholds manufactured against me.
10. The Lord should anoint me with the power to pursue, overtake and recover my stolen properties from the enemy.
11. The Lord should bring to naught every evil counselor and counsel against me.
12. The enemy shall not have a hiding place in my life in Jesus' name.

13. Let all blocked ways of prosperity be open up in Jesus' name.
14. I command the devil to take his legs off my finances in Jesus' name.
15. I paralyze every spirit of Goliath with the stones of fire in the name of Jesus.
16. Pray in the Spirit for at least fifteen (15) minutes.
17. I command every demonic transport vehicle loading away my benefits to be paralyzed, in the name of Jesus.
18. I receive the power to pursue every stubborn pursue into the red sea, in the name of Jesus.
19. Let the mandate issued to every robber of my blessing be rendered null and void, in the name of Jesus.
20. O Lord, provide me with the Moses to face my Pharaoh and the David to face my Goliath.
21. Let the wheels of all pursuing evil chariots be chattered, in the name of Jesus.
22. I pursue and overtake all forces of household wickedness and I recover my stolen items from them, in the name of Jesus.
23. Let blessings, goodness and prosperity pursue and overtake me, in the mighty name of Jesus.
24. I command all my properties captured by spiritual robbers in the dream to become too hot to handle and to come back to me, in the name of Jesus.

THE MATHEMATIC OF LIFE

Be CAREFUL of who you pick
as a FRIEND,
most people PRETEND to listen,
but are only gathering
information to JUDGE you with.

WHERE DO YOU BELONG TO
45% of people in the word today don`t know where they're going in life.
40% are happy to follow any who is ready to leads them.
12% know what they want but are not prepared to sacrifice for it. Doubts and fears constantly cripple them.
3% have clear goals in life and with determination they sacrifice for

What they believe and get what they want.
In Gideon's time, his majority were not winners neither.
The bible shows the initial turnout of 32,000 people to fight the enemies (problem), and inherit god's blessing with victories. But: 22,000 already declared it wasn't for them!
9,700 thought they could but they failed to keep faith!
300 were ready to sacrifice all and were not backing down.

GOD IS AVAILABLE
To those who are reliable
His presence, Retainable
His person, Acceptable
His power, Unmatchable
His Love, Inexplicably Immeasurable
His Grace, Undeniable
His Mercy, Unquantifiable
His Gifts, Irrevocable
The truth of His Existence, Infallible
My trust in Him, Impregnable...
Could you just imagine the Ambidextrous of my God?

A bad attitude is like a flat tire.
You can't go anywhere
until you change it.

□□□□□□□□□□□□□□□

JESUS WHY YOU REALLY NEED HIM

If you are successful in this life with materials possession, and say that you do not need Jesus. I have something to tell you. The hidden truth from such a thought I that Jesus is more than being successful in this present world knowing Jesus is the beginning of Real! Success and Joy. And do you know that you need to be successful beyond this present world? If so, Jesus is He that you need in your present life.

If and then you accept Him, the first thing you will notice instantly is joy, the type you never had before, despite your material success. Then Jesus will guard those things you term "success" or wealth in your life. In fact you shall be blessed the more in Jesus name II Timothy 1:12.

Jesus shall say you and your possessions against horrors and discovering pest of this world. Hebrew 7:25 On top of these He will fill with joy. Read 1 Sam 35, 10, 7; Psalm 16:11; Nehemiah 8:10. Jesus is the source of these and many more for you. Romans 5:11.

For those of you who are laboring in one way or the other, it is Jesus you need: This does not cost you anything than to accept and believe Him put an automatic and instant STOP to your toiling, poverty, recurring sickness, failures and other troubles by accepting Jesus. This is no joke! You people always say "Trial will convince you". Have that trial TODAY! Do not say seeing is believing. Believing first and you will see the glory of God. In line with
Hebrew 11:1. Read further the following passages Math. 1:28-30, 1 Cor. 8:9, Eph. 4:19, Jude 1.
1 Cor. 8:9

OTHER BOOKS BY THE AUTHOR

1. Sound of abundance of rain
2. How old is maturity
3. Bedrock for wedlock
4. Gods living ambassador
5. At the darkest hour
6. When miracle becomes impossible
7. Change your gear
8. Breakthroughs before day break
9. My cup running over
10. When a healer needs healing
11. Are you passing through
12. Fight to lay hold

ABOUT THE AUTHOR

Joel Odunayo Daramola whom God raised from grass to grace, has pioneered many parishes in The Redeemed Christian Church of God.

Currently: As Assistance Provincial Pastor Admin in Lagos province 37.

A graduate of The Redeemed Christian Bible College (RCBC), School of Disciple (SOD) and Institute of Leadership.

He holds a B.A. (Ed) in Guidance and Counseling from the prestigious University of Lagos (UNILAG).

He is a teacher who is registered with the teacher's registration council of Nigeria (TRCN)

A trained R & A Engineer (thermodynamics) with over 30 years' experience.

He is the CEO, Ayo-Technical Services (ATS). & Vision Link For You and I.

He is the host of Power Service (a weekly breakthrough and deliverance service) for over two decades.

A prolific writer, author of many books; a respected Evangelist, a gifted prophet with vast insight into the word of God.

Publisher of the Monthly Journal: "VISION LINK" for more than 20 years.

He has the vision to challenge young people to actualize their potentials in life.

His mandate is to spread the word of God, raise disciples, and build them to maturity for the perfection of saints through God's empowerment.

A prolific speaker, dexterous writer and a leading voice in Ministry and Leadership circles,

He is sought as a Conference speaker across the globe. His ministry is in high demand by both denominational and non-denominational ministries alike as his ability to engage people with God's word and effective prayer

He is passionate about raising people who are thoroughly steeped in Kingdom values and very relevant in the Secular world.

He believes that Christians should be able to influence society with kingdom principles.

His fine blend of excellence and spirituality has made him stand out from the pack.

He believes God has a plan for everybody and that God can take the most unlikely and use him powerfully.

A Youth leader, an administrator, entrepreneur and motivational speaker with a global vision.

A motivational speaker for over two decades. He has organized seminars and conferences to inspire the Youths in schools and Church for Nation building, Vision discovery and career advancement. His fine blend of excellence and spirituality has made him stand out from the pack, he believes that God has a plan for everybody and that God can make use of anyone powerfully.

He has published many books; Sounds of the abundance of rain; At the darkest hour; Are you passing through? Destined for greatness but tied down among others.

He is happily married to Pastor (Mrs.) C.O. Daramola and their union is blessed with four Children: Power, Queen, Excellence and Great.

Emails: pastordara@yahoo.com & visionlinkdara1@gmail.com

Phone & WhatsApp +2348033275896.

Facebook: Joel Odunayo Daramola

Websites: www.visionlink4u.com

www.ingramcontent.com/pod-product-compliance
Lightning Source LLC
LaVergne TN
LVHW012110160826
845678LV00014B/3017

* 9 7 9 8 3 6 8 2 4 6 4 7 5 *